First-Rate Reading™ ^Basics

Fluency, Vocabulary, and Comprehension

Kindergarten

by Elizabeth Suarez Aguerre

Carson-Dellosa Publishing Company, Inc. • Greensboro, North Carolina

Credits and Dedication

Project Director:

Kelly Gunzenhauser

Layout Design:

Jon Nawrocik

Inside Illustrations:

Stefano Giorgi

Cover Design:

Peggy Jackson

Cover Illustrations:

Stefano Giorgi

This book is dedicated to two amazing professors at Florida International University: Dr. Joyce Fine and Dr. Sharon Kossack. It is also dedicated to the memory of Dr. Joseph Kaplan, the professor who helped me realize that the classroom is where I am meant to be.

-E. S. A.

Table of Contents

Introduction

Kindergartners are often too young to do much independent reading. Even so, it is not too early to work with them on reading skills. Very young students love to be read to, and reading skills can be transferred to students as they listen. Most kindergarten teachers have extensive programs that deal with phonemic awareness and phonics (letter recognition, letter-sound correlation, word families, basic letter writing skills, etc.). This book focuses on fluency, vocabulary, and comprehension for kindergartners.

Some aspects of fluency are particularly difficult for kindergartners. As teachers help them read or read aloud to them, students will focus mainly on expression and sounding natural. But, if students can see the text and know that their teacher is reading each word as it appears, they learn accuracy skills at the same time. Therefore, fluency activities for kindergarten usually combine several fluency skills at once. To help inform families that reading aloud to children gives them a solid base in fluency, send home the reproducible Parent Letter: Fluency (page 5). This letter informs parents about which skills they impart to their children while reading aloud, and also offers suggestions for making the most of read-aloud experiences.

Students learn most vocabulary indirectly by having conversations, listening to stories, and reading independently. Direct vocabulary instruction helps students learn words and skills that they may not understand through indirect instruction alone. There are two main types of direct instruction. One type introduces new vocabulary words before reading. The other type teaches students how to use word-learning strategies to figure out new vocabulary words. The specific word instruction section of this book provides pre-reading activities and extended instruction. Students will learn to use reference aids, such as dictionaries and glossaries; analyze word parts; and learn how to use context clues to decipher the meanings of words. To inform families about how to help students improve their vocabulary skills, send home the reproducible Parent Letter: Vocabulary (page 6).

Finally, many reading teachers would argue that all reading instruction roads lead to comprehension. Phonemic awareness, phonics, fluency, and vocabulary are all important to learn because they assist in comprehension. Comprehension activities at this level assume that students are ready to make value judgments about the information they read, determine whether they agree or disagree with it, and also determine whether they like certain texts and make reading choices based on those likes or dislikes. Kindergartners need extra help learning to use these skills, and the activities in this book are designed to prepare young students to become discerning readers. Send home the reproducible Parent Letter: Comprehension (page 7) to explain the importance of learning comprehension skills.

Also note that the reproducible activities and the three assessment sections (pages 34–37, 54–56, and 78–80) take into account that many kindergarten students are pre-readers. When teaching, assigning reproducibles, and assessing, use your best judgment and be ready to adjust a reader activity to a nonreader activity, if needed. This may mean reading reproducible directions, letting students dictate instead of write, reading materials to students, and grouping students of different skill levels so that readers can assist nonreaders.

Name _____

Parent Letter: Fluency

Dear Parents/Family:

Research shows that good readers are more successful in school. Reading is used in all other subjects and is critical for success in real life. It is important for your child to develop a solid reading base that extends beyond phonics into other areas such as fluency. Following are suggestions and information about helping your child become a more fluent reader.

Fluency is the ability to read aloud accurately and quickly. If a reader struggles to sound out words or reads in a choppy, very slow, or unnatural way, he will not understand what he is reading as well as he could. Help your child improve his or her fluency by doing the following:

- Read aloud to your child often. Young children need to learn what fluent readers sound like. When you read aloud, read in a clear, strong voice. Read the way you speak if you are talking. Be expressive: if a character is happy, read with a happy voice. Be sure your reading is smooth, fluid, and flowing—not choppy or like a robot. Try changing your voice for different characters. You might feel silly, but your child will absolutely love this!
- Use your finger to track the print (underline words) as you read. This will help your child understand that words and sentences go together and your voice follows the text's patterns. Occasionally, have your child track the print with his or her finger.
- Echo read with your child by having your child repeat the reading after you. Your child will automatically read the text just as you do, including expression, speed, etc. When echo reading, read in short sentences or phrases so that your child can keep up. Track the print so that your child will follow the words with his or her eyes while repeating them.
- Choral read with your child (read at the same time). This works well with simple text, rhyming text, or books your child has nearly memorized. Simply tell your child to join in whenever he or she wants to.

Using these ideas will help your child begin to enjoy reading. For more information, please feel free to contact me.

Sincerely,

_____

Name _____

Parent Letter: Vocabulary

Dear Parents/Family:

Research shows that good readers are more successful in school. Reading is used in all other subjects and is critical for success in real life. It is important for your child to develop a solid reading base that extends beyond phonics into other areas such as vocabulary. Following are suggestions and information about this area of instruction.

Readers need good **vocabularies** because they must know most of the words in the text to comprehend it. Children must have good oral vocabularies (words they speak and hear) as well as written vocabularies (words they write and read). Help your child improve vocabulary skills by doing the following:

- Expose your child to many oral language experiences. Children learn a great part of their vocabulary indirectly—by being exposed to new vocabulary. Let your child engage in conversation with you and other adults, and do not use "baby talk" or "watered down" vocabulary.
- Read aloud to your child often. Include books that are above your child's reading level. Students' listening comprehension levels are higher than their reading levels, so they usually understand text that is being read to them. Pause when you come to new words to define and discuss them. Tell your child to stop you if you read words that are not familiar.
- Encourage your child to read independently as often as possible. Surround your child with literature.
- Finally, students indirectly learn vocabulary through new experiences. These experiences build what is referred to as "prior knowledge." Prior knowledge plays a major role in students' comprehension and vocabulary acquisition. Experiences can be simple or elaborate.

Using these ideas will help your child begin to enjoy reading. For more information, please feel free to contact me.

Sincerely,

_____

Name _____

Parent Letter: Comprehension

Dear Parents/Family:

Good readers are more successful in school. Reading is used in all other subjects and is critical for success in real life. It is important for your child to develop a solid reading base that extends beyond phonics into other areas, such as comprehension. Following are suggestions and information about this area of instruction.

Comprehension is the purpose for reading. It allows the reader to make connections between the text and other texts or experiences. Help your child improve comprehension by doing the following:

- Be a good reading role model. Be sure your child sees you reading often.
- Make reading a reward. Use books and reading time as a reward for good behavior, school improvement, etc.
- Take your child to the library to check out books regularly and to attend programs, such as story time, puppet shows, etc.
- An amazing feeling comes with owning books. Help your child build a home library. Create a special bookshelf and let your child earn book money by doing chores or saving allowance.
- Have a weekly or nightly "Family Reading Time." Turn off televisions, computers, and phones, and read. Read a book together, or read independently and share what you are reading about.
- Discuss what your child is reading. Ask "thinking questions," such as, "What do you think will happen next? Why do you think the character did that? How would you feel if you were the character? If you could change anything about the story, what would it be? What's happened so far?"
- Read sections of the newspaper together. Discuss the articles.
- Purchase or borrow books on tape. Have your child listen to a story and follow along with the text.
- Ask your child questions, such as, "What do you like most/least about this story? What do you think will happen next? What is this story about? What happened at the beginning/middle/end?"

Using these ideas will help your child improve reading comprehension. For more information, please feel free to contact me.

Sincerely,

_____

Fluency

Overview: Selecting Appropriate Text for Student Fluency Practice

Fluency development occurs when students have many opportunities to successfully practice their fluency. It is critical that students use text that is relatively easy for them (at their independent reading levels) so that they are not focusing on decoding words. When a student can read a text with 95% accuracy, it is at his independent reading level—the student will misread only about one out of 20 words. Therefore, if a student is reading a passage containing 20 words, he should only have difficulty with about one word. Text at 95% accuracy is appropriate for fluency practice. Instructional level text is challenging but manageable for the reader. Students will have about 90% success, misreading about one in 10 words. Instructional level text is appropriate for teaching various activities and lessons but is not appropriate for independent fluency practice. Finally, frustrating text is difficult for students. They will have less than 90% success, missing more than one in 10 words. This level of text is not appropriate for fluency practice and should only be used with a very high level of teacher guidance and support. Note that because students' reading levels vary greatly, a passage that is frustrating for one student will be at the independent reading level of another.

Literature Suggestions for Teaching Fluency

Many children's books are ideal for teaching fluency. Choose simple rhyming books or books with "sing-songy" patterns; predictable, repetitive language; and short, simple text. Below is a list of excellent choices to get you started.

Brown Bear, Brown Bear, What Do You See? by Bill Martin, Jr. (Henry Holt & Co., 1983)
Chicka Chicka Boom Boom by Bill Martin, Jr. (Simon & Schuster, 1989)
The Foot Book by Dr. Seuss (Random House, 1996)
Goodnight Moon by Margaret Wise Brown (HarperCollins, 1976)
Green Eggs and Ham by Dr. Seuss (Random House, 1960)
Hop on Pop by Dr. Seuss (Random House, 1976)
I Know an Old Lady Who Swallowed a Fly by Simms Taback (Viking, 1997)
In the Tall, Tall Grass by Denise Fleming (Henry Holt & Co., 1995)
The Napping House by Audrey Wood (Red Wagon Books, 2000)
No, David! by David Shannon (Scholastic, 1998)
One Fish, Two Fish, Red Fish, Blue Fish by Dr. Seuss (Random House, 1976)
This Is the House That Jack Built by Pam Adams (Child's Play-International, 1990)

Catch the Mistake

Set the scene by saying, "Sometimes mistakes just fly out of my mouth!" Give each student a small, foam cup and a sharpened pencil. Help each student push his pencil through the side of the cup near the opening to make a "net." Allow students to "catch" imaginary mistakes in the air by waving their nets. Next, choose a book to read aloud and explain that you may make mistakes, such as saying the wrong word or mispronouncing words. When students hear a mistake, direct them to swoop their nets to catch it. Explain that it is important for students to catch their own mistakes. If they are reading words that make no sense, they haven't caught their mistakes. Have each student read easy text to a partner and wave the net if she catches herself making mistakes. Partners should confirm whether the readers caught the mistakes. Then, let partners reverse roles.

Simple Read-Aloud

Start teaching fluency by scheduling a daily read-aloud time. Material that you read aloud to students should be slightly more difficult than students' general reading levels. This is because their speech and listening levels are higher than their reading levels, and also because they will be exposed to higher vocabulary, more complex sentence structure, and longer text patterns. First, offer a choice of books that provide the opportunity to "perform" (not informational text) and let a student choose a book each day. As you read, ask students to identify different character voices and emotions. Discuss how your voice intonations and expression make the reading more fun and interesting to listen to. Occasionally ask students what they enjoy about read-aloud time. Ask, "Do you notice how I sound like different characters with different emotions? Do you hear that I sound very natural, as if I were talking to a friend?" After you read each book, reinforce expressiveness by letting students take turns mimicking the voices you used for different characters.

Think-Aloud with Big Books

Take read-aloud sessions a step further by using a big book, so that students can clearly see your reading process. First, track the print as you read and let students follow along so that they will see how the text shows the reader when to raise or lower his voice, pause, stop, exclaim, group words together, etc. For example, when reading the book *Brown Bear, Brown Bear, What Do You See?* by Bill Martin, Jr. (Henry Holt & Co., 1983), raise your voice and stop at the end of each question, pause at the commas, group *brown* and *bear* together, etc. In addition to pointing to the text, think aloud about the oral reading process for students. Explain why you paused momentarily by saying, "See this little mark? It is a comma, and it tells me to take a little breath or pause here." Highlight raising your voice by saying, "See how the author put a question mark here? The question mark tells me that I'm supposed to raise the tone of my voice." These clues demonstrate that reading aloud is a series of conscious choices the reader makes in order to bring the text to life.

Rereading

Repeated oral readings greatly improve students' fluency by creating familiarity with text. Select appropriate text that is at the average student's independent reading level. (See page 8.) Text for rereadings should be short—about 50 words for early readers. Poetry is effective due to its rhythm, rhyme, and short text patterns, but be sure to offer a variety of reading materials for rereadings throughout the year. Model fluent reading of the chosen selection so that students will know how they should eventually sound, then have students practice reading aloud to themselves. Explain that students must read the text several times to achieve some level of fluency. Four times is sufficient for many students, but the exact number will vary. The rereadings do not have to be done on the same day and can be done in a number of ways, as demonstrated in several of the following activities.

One-on-One Reading

One-on-one instruction is not always practical or feasible, but it is an ideal setting to provide specific feedback and guidance. Schedule time to read with each student and also ask other adults, such as parents, volunteers, classroom aides, tutors, or even older, proficient students, to work directly with individual students. (See page 14 for tips about how to prepare helpers.) Instruct volunteers on how to provide feedback, such as, "The way you read every single word correctly was very impressive! That is a big part of being a fluent reader. When you reread, try to chunk your words together into phrases."

Partner/Small-Group/Choral Reading

Many arrangements give students opportunities to read with others. One simple arrangement is to have students read in pairs. It is ideal (but not absolutely necessary) to pair a less proficient reader with a more proficient one. Have students take turns reading aloud and providing feedback for each other. Another arrangement is to assign students to small groups to read together in unison, in turn, or with adults. One adult can work with a small group while another works with the rest of the class. Groups can choral read (read the same material in unison with other readers). Provide a big book for choral reading or let students use multiple copies. Predictable books with repeated text or rhyming language are particularly effective for choral reading because students will naturally want to join in, and it will be simple for them to learn the words and follow along. There is a tendency for the adult to slow down his reading and become somewhat robotic when reading chorally in order for students to keep up with the text. However, it is critical that the adult not do this because it reinforces nonfluent reading.

Tape-Assisted Reading

Tape-assisted reading is an excellent way to provide more "fluent readers" for students. Tapes eliminate the need for an actual person to work with students and can be placed in a center so that individual students or small groups can work with them. Prepare a tape by recording yourself or another fluent reader reading an appropriate passage or purchase ready-made tapes, but be sure they do not have extraneous sounds (sound effects, music, etc.). Place the tape and passage in a center. Allow students to visit the center to listen to the tape and practice reading along with the fluent reading they hear.

Readers' Theater

With readers' theater, students practice rereading text for a legitimate purpose: to present their "plays" to the class or another audience. The "scripts" can be taken directly from a simple book or story read in class, can be rewritten based on the literature, or can by found on numerous Web sites. When selecting the material, keep scripts short and simple enough for kindergarten students and make adjustments as needed. For example, narrate a story and have students read only short pieces of dialogue, or assign a group of less proficient readers to choral read text that is repeated throughout a book. In fact, it is more effective for fluency development if students read their parts rather than memorize them. Remind students to be expressive, to read in a natural manner, to speak loudly and clearly, to sound natural and realistic, and to read their parts accurately and automatically.

Rate My Readers' Theater

Have students rate performances using the Rate My Readers' Theater reproducible (page 12). First, create a transparency of the Rate My Readers' Theater reproducible, and use it to model your own rating scale of a reading performance. After another readers' theater performance, give a copy of the reproducible to each student. Explain and provide examples of each fluency aspect. Write group members' names on the board for students to copy. Read each line and give students time to answer. You may want to model your ratings at the same time until students are familiar with the reproducible, staying on a positive note so that performers do not feel embarrassed or uncomfortable. Finally, discuss students' ratings and review how students can improve in each area.

Rate My Readers' Theater

Circle the faces that match
how well you think the group did.

Group name _____

The group read their
words correctly.

The group sounded
natural and smooth.

The group
was expressive.

The group used loud and
clear voices.

First-Rate Reading™: Fluency, Vocabulary, Comprehension • CD-104017 • © Carson-Dellosa
Basics

Echo Reading: Whole Class

Echo reading, a simple but highly effective strategy, happens when a fluent reader reads a sentence (or phrase) and a developing reader repeats it (or echoes). This strategy is effective because the echoing reader will automatically repeat the text just as the fluent reader read it. If the fluent reader uses expression, voice intonations, pauses, etc., the echoing reader will echo these patterns. The most common arrangement for echo reading is with a whole class. Choose a rhyming text that is familiar to students. Be sure all students can see the text by using a big book, writing text on the board or chart paper, making multiple copies, or using an overhead projector. Students must be able to follow the text with their eyes as they echo so that they can make connections between the voice intonations, pauses, chunking of words, etc., and the text. Read the text aloud in a fluent manner and have the whole class echo read after you. When students sound "robotic" because they are trying to keep up with each other, stop and point it out so that students can self-correct. Consider taping the reading and playing the tape to alert students to any changes you want them to make.

Echo Reading: Small Groups

Assign students to small groups and prepare them to read different parts during one class reading of a familiar text, such as a fairy tale. For example, divide the class into four groups when reading *The Three Little Pigs*. Work with one group at a time to master one character's part while the other groups practice. Have one group echo read the first little pig's lines, another group echo read the second little pig's lines, etc. As you work with one group at a time, read expressively and alter your voice to match the corresponding characters so that students will do the same. When each group has practiced echo reading with you at least four times, allow all of the roles to come together into their corresponding character groups. Have each group echo as you read each character's dialogue. For further small group practice, choose one proficient reader from each group to assume your role and read each part individually while her group echo reads the text.

Echo Reading: One-on-One

One-on-one echo reading is especially helpful for struggling readers because it is a simple way to help them develop oral reading without feeling overwhelmed by the text. Individual echo reading also allows readers to focus on reading at your pace and understanding the words rather than keeping up with others. For advanced readers, use individual echo reading to fine-tune expression, rhythm, pronunciation, and character voices. Let a student choose a slightly easy text to echo read. Track the print as you read and again as the student echoes. If you do several one-on-one echo-reading sessions throughout the school year, maintain a list of each student's reading selections as a record of how he has progressed. (Students should choose slightly more difficult texts as the year progresses.)

Assisted Fluency Reading: Teacher- or Adult-Volunteer-Assisted

Although the ideal situation for helping students develop fluency is through one-on-one activities, this is often very difficult to set up. Many classrooms have so many students that one-on-one work is a management problem. Additionally, finding helpers is often challenging, but some one-on-one work should be possible. To foster a good assisted-reading environment, create a special reading corner that has a large selection of books appropriate for fluency practice, as well as special furniture, pillows, a curtain on a clothesline, or some other means to separate this area from the rest of the classroom. (If space is at a premium, add a student chair behind your desk and let each student join you there.) Have the rest of the class work on fluency development or other tasks in pairs or small groups. Select students to work with you based on who is "working nicely" or "on-task," so that the class behaves while you work with students individually. Choose one student at a time to come to the fluency corner and read with you for a few minutes. If possible, designate a simple goal for each student to work toward, such as expression or accuracy. Or, just enjoy the time listening to and helping the student read. If you have adult volunteers coming to read with students, they may need to be taught how to do this effectively. Create a simple fluency workshop for interested adults. Use explanation and role-playing to teach them how to work one-on-one with students as they practice and develop fluency, how to positively and accurately provide feedback, how to be good reading role models, etc. Use the Reading Partners reproducible (page 15) to reinforce the training. When volunteers are trained, schedule each volunteer to work with one student at a time.

Assisted Fluency Reading: Older Student- and Classmate-Assisted

Both older students and proficient classmates can help with fluency practice. To enlist help from older students, team up with a colleague who teaches a higher grade and ask her to train her class to positively praise and critique younger students. Provide copies of the Reading Partners reproducible (page 15) to help students prepare. (Cover the directions before copying.) The colleague should instruct older students to compliment younger ones on reading difficult words, reading accurately, using expression, etc. Older students should also help younger students read accurately and should point out relevant punctuation and other text effects. Let younger students choose books several days ahead of time. Have them submit a list or copies of the selections to the other teacher so that the older students can become fluent with the selections. Then, bring the classes together and pair an older student with each younger student or create a schedule for small groups of older students to work with younger ones. During the tutoring time, have older students read aloud to the kindergartners, then have the kindergartners practice rereading the passages as the tutors provide feedback. Use proficient classmates in much the same way by prepping them to be helpers or "buddies." First, listen to students read a selected passage to determine their fluency levels. When you are satisfied that these students are fluent, role-play the type of feedback, behavior, and language you expect. Because most young children tend to emulate the teacher, they will pick it up easily! Pair each helper with a less proficient reader. Have the helpers read the passage aloud, read it echo-style with their buddies, then listen to their buddies reread the text a few times until the buddies are more fluent. When they are finished reading, have helpers provide positive feedback. Explain that helpers should be able to state at least one thing that each reader did well. Provide sentence starters, such as, "You did a good job reading that because you . . ." or "I like how you . . ."

Reading Partners

Use this reproducible reference sheet for training parents, adult volunteers, and student tutors. Use the tips to help students and volunteers work together.

Fluency is the ability to read material accurately and quickly. A fluent reader can focus on comprehension instead of decoding words.

Areas of fluency:
- Accuracy—reading the words accurately, or correctly
- Automaticity—reading the words automatically, or quickly
- Expression—reading with proper expression, feeling, emotion, and voice tone
- Naturalness/smoothness/flow—reading at a proper speed, sounding natural (not choppy or robotic, but pronouncing words the way you would when speaking)

When working with developing readers:
- always be a good reading role model. You should read fluently so that others will copy you!
- use positive words and phrases like: "Good job!" "I liked the way you . . . ." "You really did a nice job when you . . . ." "That was great. Next time, try . . . ." Focus on what the reader did well and offer gentle suggestions for improvement.

Recorded Readings: Quick Practice

Recorded readings require using an audiotape to help students improve fluency. Recordings provide a developing reader with an opportunity to listen to himself read, notice what he does well and how he needs to improve, and listen to and analyze another reader's fluency. For quick, immediate practice, record a student's first read-aloud of a text. Assure the student that you expect him to struggle during a first reading. Stop the tape, allow the student to practice reading the same text about four times, then record him reading aloud again. Play back the first attempt and discuss what he had trouble with and what he did well. Then, play the second recording and compare the two. Help the student identify what changed during the second recording and why. Talk about how practice clearly improves fluency.

Recorded Readings: Fluency Self-Analysis

This simple, open-ended activity gives students opportunities to hear themselves as readers. They will often notice if they sound "funny," too slow, too fast, or even boring! It is also an excellent assessment tool. Record the student reading aloud a familiar passage. Play the tape for the student as she tracks the text. After she listens, ask, "Did you make any errors? How did you sound? Were you expressive? Was your voice loud and clear? Did you "chunk" the words? Did you sound natural—or choppy, like a robot?" Consider keeping the tape to record the same student reading throughout the year. Periodically let the student play her past readings and note improvements and changes.

Recorded Readings: Listen to the Teacher

Record yourself reading a familiar passage. Be sure to make a few errors, such as reading a word inaccurately, chopping up the words to sound robotic or unnatural, speeding up or slowing down too much, overpronouncing words (such as *pret-ty* with an overemphasis on the middle /t/ phoneme), or ignoring punctuation. Do not make too many errors in one recording; the errors should stand out. Then, replay the tape for small groups, individuals, or the whole class, as each student views the text. Ask students to identify the errors. If they have copies of the text that they can write on, consider having students circle or underline the words you mispronounce. When a student identifies a fluency mistake, ask him to be specific. For example, if a student says: "You sounded funny," ask, "How did I sound funny? What do you mean by funny? What part sounded funny?" Also, ask for suggestions about what you can do to improve your next reading, such as reading faster or more slowly, tracking the print with your finger, etc.

First-Rate Reading™: Fluency, Vocabulary, Comprehension • CD-104017 • © Carson-Dellosa
Basics

Let's Talk about Chunking

Chunking refers to the natural grouping of words into phrases when reading fluently. Chunking gives text its rhythm. Young readers tend to read in a choppy, word-by-word manner because they are so focused on decoding words when reading aloud. Many primary literature books are excellent resources for teaching chunking because the text is naturally written in phrases or "chunks." See literature suggestions (page 8) for ideas. Big books are especially effective to use for practice with this skill because all students can see you point to the text as it is being read in a rhythm. When reading aloud from a big book, point to the text and pause to discuss how you group words together as you read aloud. For example, while reading *Panda Bear, Panda Bear, What Do You See?* by Bill Martin, Jr. (Henry Holt & Co., 2003), say, "See how the animal words are grouped together on the same page—*panda bear, bald eagle* . . . ? Did you hear how I read them together? That's because they go together. Wouldn't it sound funny if I read them like this: *panda* (pause) *bear panda* (pause) *bear?*" Let students practice chunking correctly and incorrectly to hear the difference.

Chunking and Tracking

Have students point to the text in a big book or on a piece of chart paper while you read aloud to help them experience the natural chunking of words in a kinesthetic way. When students are reading aloud, remind them to point to the words, too. Because of the natural tendency to tap their fingers from word to word, students often slow down their reading to a choppy pace. Instead, encourage them to "slide" their fingers from word to word. Have students practice by asking them to track the print for each other when working in pairs.

Chunking with the Fat Cat

Use the Chunking with the Fat Cat reproducible (page 18) to practice chunking. Read the first poem aloud once as students follow along on their copies or the overhead projector. Read it a second time and "chunk" phrases as students echo. Next, read it chorally with students. Ask which words are chunked, or "go together." Point out how the words are written to help the reader be fluent by sounding natural, not choppy or robotic. Have students take turns reading the poem with partners. Remind students that they should be chunking, or grouping, the words together so that they "sound right." Use the second poem as a follow up, practice, extension, or assessment. Model fluently reading the poem before having students attempt it independently.

Chunking with the Fat Cat

Read the poems below. "Chunk" the words into phrases so that they sound natural. Practice the reading at least four times.

The fat cat

sat on the hat.

The hat went flat.

"Meow, meow!" said the cat.

The white dog barks.

The green bird sings.

The orange cat meows.

The yellow lion roars.

Word Card Reading for Chunking Practice

Provide students with a different kinesthetic method to practice chunking. Copy familiar story words onto index cards (one word per card) that form a sentence or phrase when read together, such as *panda, bear, panda, bear, what, do, you,* and *see.* Have a volunteer hold each word card. Arrange students in the correct order, standing a few feet apart from each other. Ask the class to read each word card, pausing between cards. The reading will sound choppy and unrelated. Then, have the two students holding *panda* and *bear* link arms and stand closely together. Repeat with the next two cards (*panda, bear*) and again with *what, do, you,* and *see* so that you will have three groups of students linked together. Have the class read the word cards again, this time grouping, or "chunking," the linked students' word cards. The reading will now sound more fluent and related. Ask students which way sounded better and made more sense. After they say that the second way sounded better, explain that this is because part of reading is being fluent and reading words in a way that makes sense. The word cards for *panda* and *bear,* as well as the word cards *what, do, you,* and *see,* belong together because that is the way students should fluently read that phrase. Repeat this activity several times with new sets of word cards. Each time, have different students sort themselves into the appropriate groups. Encourage students without cards to participate by helping the volunteers chunk themselves correctly and by chorally reading the cards. Create word cards according to students' reading levels, decoding skills, and the literature with which they are familiar. Students can also practice chunking using the word cards independently or in a center. Show students how to place the word cards in the correct order, read each word independently, then slide the cards together to form a chunked sentence. Students should go from reading in a choppy, abrupt manner with the individual word cards to combining the words into a more fluent, smooth sentence or phrase.

Read to the Rhythm

Give students a fun opportunity to use their bodies and musical abilities when developing fluency. This activity works particularly well with text that is naturally rhythmic, such as simple poetry, rhyming books, chants, and nursery rhymes. Select a very familiar passage, poem, or book. If possible, give each student an instrument, such as a tambourine, cymbals, percussion sticks, etc. Have students "play" their instruments to the rhythm of the text as they read. If instruments are not available, have students clap, stomp, march, tap, or even jump to the rhythm of the text. This will help students "feel" and "see" the rhythm of fluent reading.

Using a Language Experience Approach to Practice Fluency

The term "language experience approach" (LEA) refers to having students dictate "stories" about an experience or activity, such as a field trip, assembly, or any other experience. LEA is an excellent technique for fluency practice because students read their own language and word choices, and the topics are personal. Give the whole class a few minutes to dictate a story to you, one sentence per student. Record the sentences on a piece of chart paper. After the dictation is complete, read the text back to students in order to familiarize them with it in printed format. Then, let the class practice together, individually, and in small groups to chorally read, echo read, reread, etc. After students have practiced, give each student or small group a chance to read the text in front of the class. Let the most proficient readers go first so that less proficient readers can hear the text several times before reading. Repeat this activity with new stories until each student or small group has told a story.

Language Experience Approach and Student Drawings

Very young and beginning writers are often able to draw better than they can write and may feel more confident explaining drawings than dictating stories. Also, when they have visual prompts, students may need less prodding to describe things and create enough text for reading experiences. Readers will benefit from this activity, and pre-readers will be able to use the experience to learn to read fluently. Ask each student to draw a picture of something she did recently with her family, such as take a trip, have a nice meal, celebrate a holiday, etc. Then, sit with each student as she dictates sentences about what her picture represents. Write what the student says and help her read it back. Over a few days, work with each student to reread her sentences. As students learn to read the words without decoding them and become more comfortable with the reading, allow them to read their sentences and show their drawings to the class. Extend this activity by posting all student drawings on a bulletin board. Before a parents' night or open house, tape each student's writing to her desk. Let families who attend try to match the writing to the drawings on the bulletin board.

Student Writing and Fluency: Overview

When incorporating writing activities, keep these things in mind. Many early readers still use invented spelling, which is appropriate because students will know what they meant to write. Students may continue to dictate to you, a parent volunteer, or an older student (see Language Experience Approach and Student Drawings, page 20). This is effective because even though the student has not done the actual writing, the text is still his own. After a writing activity is complete, have an adult or proficient student reader help each child read his writing once. Many young students forget what they wrote or dictated. After the initial reading, each student should practice rereading her text aloud several times until she is more fluent.

Student Writing and Fluency: Journals

Students' oral reading is usually better when they read things they wrote because their own writing is familiar, personal, and in context. Students should be prompted to write about specific things, such as stories they are reading, experiences they have had, etc. (Kindergartners are too young to "just write about anything.") One easy way to prompt students to write and then read is to assign simple journal entries. Read a new story to the class. Have each student write or dictate a journal entry in response. Give students a prompt, such as *My favorite*  *part was . . . , I like the story because . . . , I don't like the story because . . . , I thought it was funny when . . . , This story made me feel . . . ,* etc. Make sure students know that they will be sharing their journal entries aloud. Wait until the following day to have students share so that they can practice reading before sharing. The next day, before having volunteers share, reread the story to refresh students' memories. After each volunteer reads, pause to discuss both the content and fluency of her response.

Student Writing and Fluency: Greeting Cards

Have each student create and write a holiday or other type of greeting card to a family member or friend. December is a good time to do this because most students can choose holidays they celebrate in that month or the next. Have students include their favorite things about the holidays in the cards. Allow time for students to design and write their cards. Provide envelopes for students to use to enclose their cards and make sure that they address the envelopes. Then, have students take turns reading their cards and addresses aloud.

Student Writing and Fluency: Letters

Writing and reading letters is good fluency practice. Letters create a real audience for the writing. Have students write or dictate letters to their families about pertinent subjects. For example, after a field trip, let students write about their experiences. Have students read their letters aloud to partners or small groups for practice. Then, let each student take a turn reading his letter to you. Finally, send letters home with a note asking families to let students read their letters aloud. Students may also write letters to story characters, classmates, a new student, etc.

Student Writing and Fluency: Personal Narrative

Students are familiar with narrative before they learn to write it because many of their stories are narratives. Have each student write or dictate a narrative about a personal experience, such as having a pet, taking a family vacation, etc. Ask each student to bring in an object to go with her narrative, such as a treat from the field trip, a souvenir T-shirt, a pet collar, etc. Have students practice reading their narratives at least four times. Then, ask a volunteer to stand in front of the class and explain his object. After he is comfortable talking in front of the class, ask him to read his narrative.

Student Writing and Fluency: Poetry Practice

Poetry, either from books with rhyming text or children's poetry, is an excellent tool for fluency activities because of its rhythm, text structure, and rhyming patterns. Students naturally want to join in reading poetry because of its patterns and predictability. This makes it a highly motivating tool as well as "safe" text for students. Select a poem and model a first reading, then incorporate any of the following suggestions:

- Have students read the poem by groups. For example, divide the class into the number of stanzas or lines in the poem, and assign each group a section.
- Have the boys read one section and the girls read another.
- Ask student volunteers to read the poem aloud to the class.
- Have students act out the poem or move to its rhythm as they read it.
- Pair students and have them take turns reading the poem to each other.
- Send the poem home and have students practice reading it to family members. Use the poem and letter on the Poetry Practice reproducible (page 23) to have students practice their fluency at home.

Because of many poems' "sing-songy" patterns, many readers tend to read poems in a choppy, sing-songy way. Point out that this is not part of being a natural-sounding, fluent reader and correct as needed. Give examples, such as showing how to read and pause using punctuation cues rather than the end-of-line cues.

Poetry Practice

Dear Parents/Family,

Fluency, an important part of reading instruction, refers to reading text aloud in a natural, accurate, and automatic manner. A fluent reader can focus on comprehension instead of decoding words. Poetry is excellent for fluency practice because children love rhythm and rhyming patterns. Help your child's fluency development with the poem below.

- First, read the poem aloud so that your child can hear what a good reader sounds like.
- Discuss how the poem makes you feel.
- Have your child follow along as you read by pointing to the words. Talk about how question marks and exclamation points help you read more fluently by telling you where to raise the tone of your voice or speak more loudly.
- Echo read the poem with your child. (Read a line and have your child repeat it.)
- Choral read the poem. (Read the poem in unison.)
- Listen to your child read the poem aloud several times. Praise fluent reading skills, such as reading every word accurately; reading every word automatically without getting "stuck;" reading with expression; reading with a clear, loud voice; and reading in a natural, smooth manner.

Please cut out the poem and have your child bring it to school on _____ . Student volunteers will read the poem aloud to the class to demonstrate fluency.

Thank you!

Sincerely,

Reading books is so much fun!
Can you please, please read me one?
Books can make you happy.
Books can make you glad.
Books can even make you sad.
I like to read books about kids like me.
I like to read books, don't you see?
Reading books is so much fun!
Can you please, please read me one?

Thumbs-Up, Thumbs-Down

Play this game with struggling readers or students who have just begun to develop fluency. Have students practice identifying good reading and not-so-good reading. Show students "thumbs-up" and "thumbs-down," and explain what they mean. Explain that as you read aloud, students should indicate with thumbs-up or thumbs-down whether you are reading fluently. Either have students listen for overall fluent reading or have them focus on specific areas of fluency, such as appropriate speed. For example, tell students, "I am going to read now. Show me with a thumbs-up sign if I am reading just right. Show me a thumbs-down sign if I am reading too fast or too slowly." Begin reading text aloud and watch to see whether students are indicating correctly. Change between fluent and nonfluent reading so that students will have to listen carefully and change between thumbs-up and thumbs-down. For example, begin reading in a natural, fluid manner. (Students should indicate thumbs-up.) Then, slow down to a choppy, robotic manner. (Students should indicate thumbs-down.) After the teacher-led part of the activity, group students and have one student in each group read aloud while the other students indicate a thumbs-up or thumbs-down. Select readers who are already somewhat fluent so that nonfluent reading is done purposely, not because a student is simply not fluent enough. If you do not have enough fluent students, enlist help from older students or adult volunteers.

Reading Is Like Walking

Help students become more aware of the speed fluent readers should use. This activity is especially effective for students who learn from movement. Demonstrate how silly it would sound if someone spoke very slowly or very quickly rather than at a natural speed. Give students an opportunity to demonstrate, as well. Then, tell students that reading is like walking. Ask students to demonstrate how they walk. Give students an opportunity to walk around the room. Then, direct students to walk in slow motion, as if they are covered in sticky honey or glue. Ask students if this feels or looks natural. Compare this to the extra-slow talking done previously. Then, have students walk (not run) quickly. Ask students if this feels or looks normal. Tell students that they will listen to you read aloud at different speeds. When you read normally, or in a fluent manner, have students demonstrate by walking at a normal pace. When you read too quickly or too slowly, have students indicate this by speeding up or slowing down their walking.

Character Voices

Help students practice fluency using various character voices. Select a story that would be effective for implementing character voices, such as *The Three Little Pigs*, *Goldilocks and the Three Bears*, etc. Ask students how they think a particular character's voice might sound and let them demonstrate. Model the use of character voices when reading the story aloud for the first time. Then, have students read the characters' parts using appropriate voices. This can be done as a class, with all students chorally reading the part of a particular character, or students can read different character parts with corresponding voices. This activity will help students become aware of sounding expressive while reading.

Over-Pronouncing

Many young readers pronounce words phonetically—the way they learned them—while reading. A common example is that students will say "lit-tle" with the hard emphasis on the medial *t's*, making the word sound choppy. Display words on the board, such as *mitten*, *kitten*, *curtain*, *ladder*, *party*, and *butter*. If possible, include simple pictures to help students identify the words. Ask students to sound out the words with you. When students do this ("mit-ten"), say: "Yes, this is *mit-ten*, but when you say this word when you are talking, do you say *mit-ten* or *mitten*?" Explain that even though it is appropriate to "chop up" a word when trying to sound it out, it is important to pronounce the word fluently while reading—like they would say it when talking to friends. Program sentence strips with sentences containing the example words, such as *I put on my new mittens*. Help students read the sentences fluently without chopping or over-pronouncing the words. Revisit this activity when students over-pronounce during reading.

Word Attack Strategies

Many students freeze when they come to unknown words while reading aloud. Teach word attack strategies so that early readers will understand how to maintain accuracy and automaticity while reading. Ask students to offer suggestions about what to do when they come to unknown words while reading aloud. (Most will immediately suggest, "Ask the teacher/parent/someone.") To guide them toward providing other solutions, ask, "What else can you do? Can you look at the first letter? How does that help you?" Use copies of the Word Attack Strategies reproducible (page 26) to explain these strategies. Discuss the reproducible, model the strategies, and let students practice in small groups. For example, select a phrase or sentence from a current book that includes a difficult word. Model saying the beginning sound of the word, reading the rest of the text and going back to the word, guessing what would make sense, looking at the pictures for clues, etc. Let each student color the reproducible and keep it for reference, or enlarge it for use as a poster in the classroom. Give students other examples for practice. Try to refer to the reproducible often when reading so that students can practice with actual text.

Word Attack Strategies

Look at this page to help you
remember what to do when you are reading and come to a word
you don't know.

When I don't know a word, this is what I can do.

1. Say the beginning sound,
   then sound out the rest.

2. Look at the pictures to get a clue.

3. Skip it and read on.

4. Think and guess.

First-Rate Reading™: Fluency, Vocabulary, Comprehension • CD-104017 • © Carson-Dellosa
Basics

So Many Sight Words

Automatic sight word recognition is an important part of fluency development. The teaching of sight words, or high-frequency words, such as *is, what, the, with,* etc., is critical because many of these words do not have concrete meanings. Students need to automatically recognize these words in isolation and within text. Send home copies of the So Many Sight Words reproducible (page 28) (with the directions covered) and the Parent Letter: Sight Words reproducible (page 29) to help students work on them at home. Use some or all of the following strategies for teaching these words.

- Create a word wall of sight words.
- Select one sight word and count how often it appears in text. Consider creating a simple bar graph of several sight words counted in a story, such as *the, is, a, what, for, of, and,* etc.
- Write sight words on index cards and randomly distribute them to students. Read the words and have students repeat. As you read a story aloud, tell students to hold up their word cards when they hear or see their words appear in the text.
- Have students practice "writing" the sight words at a center in a variety of ways: in sand, with yarn, on a small chalkboard or write-on/wipe-away board, with dry beans, etc.
- Give students magazines or newspapers and have them highlight selected sight words.
- Prepare a center with a list of sight words and several children's books. Have each student select one sight word and tally how often it appears in one of the books.
- Write several sentences on the board or chart paper with blank lines replacing some of the sight words. (For example: ___ *girl ran in* ___ *park. She played* ___ *a ball.*) Have students refer to a displayed list of sight words and select the missing words. Ask volunteers to write the missing words on the blanks.

So Many Sight Words

Use this list as a reference when teaching sight words and to send home with the parent letter on page 29.

a	from	me	tell
after	fun	my	that
all	get	new	the
am	girl	nice	them
and	give	night	there
animal	go	no	they
are	good	not	thing
at	had	of	this
be	has	off	to
because	have	old	under
best	he	on	up
big	her	out	us
boy	here	over	very
brother	him	people	want
but	his	play	was
can	house	pretty	we
can't	how	quit	went
car	I	ride	what
children	in	run	when
come	is	said	where
day	it	saw	who
did	jump	school	why
do	kick	see	will
down	like	she	with
eat	little	sister	won't
favorite	look	some	yes
for	made	talk	you
friend	make	teacher	your

First-Rate Reading™: Fluency, Vocabulary, Comprehension • CD-104017 • © Carson-Dellosa
Basics

Parent Letter: Sight Words

Dear Parents/Family:

Sight words are words that students should automatically recognize in print. Learning sight words improves fluency because the reader does not need to pause to decode or sound out words. By reading automatically and accurately, the reader can focus on comprehension. Because many sight words do not have concrete meanings, students must simply learn them in context. For example, it is difficult to tell a child what the word *the* means. In addition to the class work your child does to learn sight words, you can help at home. Attached is a list of common sight words. Use this list in the following ways:

- Each night, take a few moments to read over the list with your child. Point to each word as you read it and have your child echo read it after you.
- Challenge your child to find one or more sight words in a newspaper, book, or magazine. Count how many times your child finds the words.
- Make a small sandbox at home for your child to practice "writing" sight words. Fill a shoe box or other similar container with about 2" (5 cm) of sand. Have your child "write" the sight words in the sand using his or her finger.
- Keep track of the sight words your child learns by putting a check beside the words he or she can read independently. Consider rewarding your child with a sticker or similar prize when he or she learns an entire row.
- Write simple sentences using some of the sight words, such as *The girl is in the house.* Ask your child to identify the sight words and help him or her read the sentence.

Feel free to contact me for more ideas. Thank you for your help!

Sincerely,

_____

Reproducible Passages to Practice Specific Fluency Skills

It can be especially challenging to practice specific fluency skills with young students because many have not mastered reading even simple text. But, it is still important to teach these skills to pre-readers. Any text used for fluency practice must be easy to read and predictable. The following reproducibles (pages 31–33) are designed to cover specific fluency skills, such as pausing appropriately for punctuation, demonstrating characters' emotions in dialogue, using text clues to adjust voice intonations, etc. The passages can be used in class and at home. Make a copy for each student and use it for fluency activities listed previously, such as rereadings, partner readings, etc. Or, make a transparency, enlarge a copy to poster size, or copy it onto chart paper. When sending the reproducible home for practice, include the parent letter that goes with each passage.

Begin working with each passage with a quick and simple pre-reading activity. Read each passage aloud fluently. Then, point out the specific skills covered in each passage. Finally, give students an opportunity to practice reading the passages with partners, in groups, one-on-one with you, to the class, etc. Remind students to copy what you did for each passage.

Use the following guidelines when using these passages in class:

Punctuation Passage (page 31)
- Content: Ask students if they have ever been to a farm or zoo. If so, ask what kinds of animals they have seen there or could expect to see.
- Fluency: Show students the commas. Tell them that these "little marks" are called commas and that commas tell the reader to pause for a little breath. Discuss how it would not sound "right" if you read the passage without the commas. (You would sound rushed and out of breath, unnatural, etc.) Repeat for the periods. Have volunteers find and count the commas, then the periods.

Dialogue Passage (page 32)
- Content: Ask students to share some foods they do not like and discuss how they would feel if someone tried to convince them to eat things they do not like. Have them name some foods they like that others may not.
- Fluency: Explain that this passage contains dialogue, which is when people are talking to each other in a story. Show the quotation marks (they look like two upside-down commas) and explain that these marks tell the reader that there is dialogue, or talking. Point out how you read the passage using the same expression you would use if you were really talking to someone in person. Point out the exclamation points and question marks. Discuss and explain them in a similar manner.

Text Clues Passage (page 33)
- Content: Ask students if they have ever played musical instruments. Ask if students know what kinds of sounds specific musical instruments make, such as violins, bassoons, etc.
- Fluency: Point out how some words are written in all uppercase letters. Ask students why they think these words are written like this. Model how to raise your voice at these points. Discuss how the capitalized words tell the reader to read these parts in a louder voice. Review exclamation points.

First-Rate Reading™: Fluency, Vocabulary, Comprehension • CD-104017 • © Carson-Dellosa
Basics

Punctuation Passage

Dear Parents/Family:

Fluency, an important part of reading instruction, refers to reading aloud in an accurate, automatic, and natural way. An important part of fluency is pausing at appropriate places. The passage below contains commas and periods that tell readers when to pause. Your child is already familiar with the passage. Here is what you can do to help:

- Read the passage to your child so that he or she can hear a good, fluent reader. Be sure to pause at the commas and periods.
- Point to the text as you read so that your child will follow along with his or her eyes.
- Read the passage chorally (at the same time) with your child. Take turns pointing to the text.
- Have your child read the passage aloud several times. Praise your child when he or she reads it accurately and pauses appropriately. Tell your child what he or she can do to improve. For example, "You did a great job! Next time, take a little breath when you see these commas. Remember that commas tell you to pause, or stop, for a moment."
- Ask your child to point out the commas in the passage. Ask him or her what the commas tell the reader to do. Repeat with periods. Ask your child to explain the difference between a comma and a period. (A comma is inside a sentence and tells the reader to take a tiny breath or pause. A period is at the end of a sentence and tells the reader to take a longer breath or pause a bit longer.)

Thank you for your cooperation!

Sincerely,

_____

- -

I Saw Many Animals

I went to a farm.

I saw many animals.

I saw cows, ducks, horses, and goats.

I went to the zoo.

I saw many animals.

I saw bears, lions, monkeys, and giraffes.

Dialogue Passage

Dear Parents/Family:

Fluency, an important part of reading instruction, refers to reading aloud in an accurate, automatic, and natural way. An important part of fluency is reading dialogue with expression. The passage below contains dialogue, question marks, and exclamation points. Your child is already familiar with the passage. Here is what you can do to help:

- Read the passage to your child so that he or she can hear a good, fluent reader. Raise your voice at the appropriate places to demonstrate the characters' emotions and use appropriate voice intonations to indicate you have read a question.
- Point to the text as you read so that your child will follow along with his or her eyes.
- Read the passage chorally (at the same time) with your child. Take turns pointing to the text.
- Have your child read the passage to you several times. Praise your child when he or she reads it accurately and with appropriate expression. Tell your child what he or she can do to improve. For example, "You did a great job! Next time, think about how you would sound if someone were trying to convince you to eat something you don't like. Read it the way you would sound when talking."
- Ask your child to point out the exclamation points and question mark in the passage. Ask him or her what these marks tell the reader to do.
- Ask your child what foods he or she likes and dislikes. Talk about what foods your child might want to try. Talk about why it is important to read dialogue the way it would sound in real life.

Thank you for your cooperation!

Sincerely,

_____

- - - - - - - - - - - - - - - - - - -

Green Apples

"Do you like green apples?" asked Jane.

"Oh, no, I do not like green apples!" said Jack.

"You should try green apples," said Jane.

"No! I do not want to try green apples!" said Jack.

"Green apples are good," said Jane.

"No! I do not want green apples!" said Jack.

"I like green apples. Green apples are good!" said Jane.

Text Clues Passage

Dear Parents/Family:

Fluency, an important part of reading instruction, refers to reading aloud in an accurate, automatic, and natural way. An important part of fluency is using the written clues to read expressively. The passage below contains words in all uppercase letters and exclamation points to indicate that the reader should raise his or her voice. Your child is already familiar with the passage. Here is what you can do to help:

- Read the passage to your child so that he or she can hear a good, fluent reader. Be sure to read the words in all caps loudly and add appropriate excitement where there are exclamation points.
- Point to the text as you read so that your child will follow along with his or her eyes.
- Read the passage chorally (at the same time) with your child. Take turns pointing to the text.
- Have your child read the passage to you several times. Praise your child when he or she reads it accurately and with appropriate voice intonations. Tell your child what he or she can do to improve. For example, "You did a great job! Next time, raise your voice when you come to a word in uppercase letters. Remember that when the whole word is written in uppercase letters like that, it tells the reader to say it loudly."
- Ask your child to point out the exclamation points and words written in all uppercase letters. Ask him or her what these clues tell the reader to do.
- Ask your child what other instruments might sound like. Have fun thinking of different noise words.

Thank you for your cooperation!

Sincerely,

_____

- -

Listen to the Band Play

Did you hear the band play?

The drum went boom, boom, BOOM!

The horn went waa, waa, WAA!

The flute went hoo, hoo, HOO!

The violin strings went zip, zip, ZIP!

Did you hear the band play?

The band played VERY LOUDLY!

Fluency Assessments

Throughout the year, it is important to assess students' fluency to ensure that they are making adequate progress and to gather critical information to help you adjust your lessons according to students' needs. Informal assessment occurs whenever you listen to students read orally and make judgments about their progress. However, more formal measures should also be included. Calculating the rate of words correct per minute is perhaps the easiest way to formally assess fluency, but depending on students' reading levels, this may or may not be a practical assessment tool. Students must be able to read at least some text with success. If students are not yet able to decode a sufficient amount of text for this assessment, try again later in the year. To complete this assessment, take timed samples of students' reading and compare the results with published oral reading fluency norms or standards. Select two or three short, grade-level passages, such as text from a basal reader or other adopted grade-level resources. Make a copy of each student's text so that you can mark on the text as a student reads. Have each student read a passage aloud for exactly one minute. Mark all errors on your copy, then subtract the total number of errors from the total number of words read to find the words correct per minute. Repeat the test two more times and determine the average.

To do a simple oral reading analysis, have each student read a passage to you. The passage should either be familiar from use in class or simple enough for each student to decode. As the student reads aloud, listen for and document various areas of fluency development. For example, mark errors, long pauses, etc., on a copy of the text. Use these results and observations as a guide to help individual students develop. Consider recording students' reading to provide evidence of their developing fluency and growth. It will serve as excellent documentation for parent conferences, as well as motivation for students to be able to hear their improvement throughout the year.

In addition to the above assessments, use the reproducibles on pages 35–37 for several forms of assessments. These are self-explanatory and can be tailored to suit each student. Even good readers will benefit from specific skill practice.

Name: Chandra Wilkinson
Date: September 14, 2006

Fluency Assessment #1

After listening to a student read aloud, record information below. Use a rating of 1-3 to assess fluency.
1=reads smoothly and with good expression, pausing when appropriate
2=somewhat fluent (exhibits some fluency characteristics but needs to improve on others)
3=choppy, uneven reading, pauses inappropriately, sounds "robotic."

Fluency Rating: 2

Reading Selection Title: The Little Red Hen

Comments: Chandra does well with her pauses, her automaticity, and her pace. She needs to improve on expression. It is hard to tell differences between characters, and her voice does not change with punctuation. When she masters this, she will be a lovely reader.

Suggestions for Practice: Chandra will listen to several books on tape, then she will explain how she could tell the differences between characters. She will practice this by recording herself reading. Next, we will work on punctuation by having Chandra write sentences and use different punctuation according to the content of each sentence. Finally, she will reread the same book selection for her next assessment.

Name _____

Date _____

Fluency Assessment #1

After listening to a student read aloud,
record information below. Use a rating of 1–3 to assess fluency.
1=reads smoothly and with good expression, pausing when appropriate
2=somewhat fluent (exhibits some fluency characteristics but needs to improve on others)
3=choppy, uneven reading, pauses inappropriately, sounds "robotic"

Fluency Rating:_____

Reading Selection Title: _____

Comments: _____

_____

_____

_____

_____

_____

_____

Suggestions for Practice: _____

_____

_____

_____

_____

_____

_____

Name _____

Date _____

Fluency Assessment #2

Once upon a time . . .

Have each student read aloud
from a story or passage he or she is currently reading in
class. Circle Yes, No, or Partial to monitor the student's fluency
development and progress.

Reading Selection Title: _____

1. Student can chorally read a section of the book with you.
   Yes   No   Partial

2. Student can point to text appropriately as you read it aloud.
   Yes   No   Partial

3. When asked, student can identify spaces between words.
   Yes   No   Partial

4. Student knows what spaces are for (pauses, take a breath, etc.).
   Yes   No   Partial

Comments: _____

_____

_____

_____

_____

_____

Name _____   *Fluency*

Date _____

Fluency Assessment #3

Have each student read a passage
aloud to you. Be sure the passage is familiar to the student. Assess
the student's fluency by circling Yes, No, or Somewhat, then add
comments below.

Reading Selection Title: _____

1. The student's voice was loud and clear.
     Yes   No   Somewhat

2. The student read almost every word accurately.
     Yes   No   Somewhat

3. The student sounded natural, not choppy.
     Yes   No   Somewhat

4. The student paused appropriately at punctuation.
     Yes   No   Somewhat

5. The student read with expression.
     Yes   No   Somewhat

Comments: _____

_____

_____

_____

Vocabulary: Indirect Instruction

Although teachers must plan specific direct word instruction, students learn the meanings of most words indirectly through daily experiences with oral and written language. Although these experiences are indirect and informal, teachers still need to make a conscious effort to include such opportunities for students in the daily curriculum.

Engaging Daily in Oral Language

Young students acquire vocabulary through conversation. Especially as they engage in conversations with adults, students hear and indirectly learn the meanings of new words. The more oral language experiences they have, the more new words students learn. Engage students in authentic, interesting conversations daily. These conversations can be based on current lessons. However, if encouraged, young students will initiate conversations with you and other adults about an endless number of topics. When this happens, resist the urge to cut the conversation short in order to go on with "real" learning activities. These conversations will often take no more than a few minutes and are of great educational value to students. When talking with students, do not simplify language so that they will understand. Use the same language you would use with adults—within reason—and define new words or provide synonyms when necessary. If, for example, you are discussing a student's recent trip to the zoo over the weekend, you might say, "When I was a child, I always loved visiting the aviary at the zoo. That's the area where all of the birds are."

Another excellent way to indirectly expose students to new vocabulary is to purposely use interesting language. For example, when getting students ready for lunch, say, "I'm glad it is lunchtime. I'm really famished and can't wait to eat!" This practice does not take up any additional class time and makes a great impact on students' vocabulary acquisition.

Read-Aloud Time

Research supports a need for daily classroom read-aloud time. This read-aloud time is a big part of indirect vocabulary instruction. Students learn new words from listening to adults read to them. Some read-aloud literature should be "just for fun" and not based on specific lessons. It should also be higher than students' independent reading levels since their listening comprehension levels are often much higher than their instructional comprehension levels. To help students understand many new words through the context of the literature, pause while reading to quickly define them. After read-aloud, relate new words and concepts to students' prior knowledge and experiences. For example, if you are reading *Freckle Juice* by Judy Blume (Yearling, 1978) aloud to students, explain that *freckles* are small, brown spots on someone's face and a *recipe* is a written plan to cook something. Ask students to look at partners to see if they have freckles. Then, ask if anyone has ever helped prepare a recipe at home and if so, have students describe the experience.

Create a Print-Rich Environment

Students should be surrounded by print. This exposure will help students acquire and learn new vocabulary words indirectly. Below are ideas for creating a print-rich environment:

- Label things around the classroom. Use sentence strips or index cards to label *door, clock, closet, window, computer, teacher's desk, shelf*, etc. Laminate these cards for durability and reuse them each year.
- Create a center at which students can look through magazines and newspapers to interact with words. Let students cut out the words to create word collages, highlight words with specific letters, etc.
- Create and maintain a word wall. The word wall can be based on phonics lessons learned throughout the year, vocabulary words learned during lessons, or any other criteria you select.
- Create a bulletin board on which students can display recognizable words from labels or brand-name products, such as cereal names, store names from ads, candy names from wrappers, etc. Have students cut them out, bring them in, and read them to the class.
- Display a bulletin board or poster with students' first and last names and birth dates.
- If students draw pictures for you, encourage them to add text (even if it is only their names or your name copied from elsewhere). Use these papers to motivate students to write notes for you to display.
- Display pertinent class information, such as the schedule, morning directions, fire drill procedures, class rules, etc., and refer to it often.
- Display class news, such as important events, exciting news, upcoming holidays, etc.

Independent Reading Time

Another way students indirectly learn vocabulary words is through independent reading time. The more students read on their own, the more words they encounter and learn. Of course, many kindergartners will not be able to read independently, but independent reading can also include rereadings of familiar text and stories first encountered in class. Students will develop their independent reading skills as they grow as readers and as they are exposed to literature and text. Encourage independent reading time at this young age by including a 5–10 minute silent sustained reading time in class, during which each student should read books of her choice. Even students who are not yet able to decode and comprehend independently will benefit from practicing reading behavior.

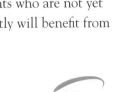

Vocabulary: Direct Instruction

Direct vocabulary instruction can be divided into two categories. *Specific word instruction* teaches individual words. This type of vocabulary instruction is important because it extends students' knowledge of word meanings and helps them understand what they are hearing or reading. It can also help them use new words accurately when writing or speaking. Specific word instruction includes the teaching of specific words, pre-reading, actively engaging students with vocabulary so that they are working and using the new words, and repeatedly exposing students to vocabulary in many contexts—not just within text. *Word learning strategies* teach students how to determine the meanings of words that are new to them without specific instruction. This type of vocabulary instruction is important because it is not possible for teachers to provide instruction for all new words students will encounter. Word learning strategies include the use of dictionaries and other reference materials, structural analysis, and context clues.

Specific Word Instruction: Vocabulary Bingo

The programmable Bingo Card reproducible (page 41) can be used a number of ways for fun vocabulary instruction, practice, review, and even assessment.

- Give young students opportunities to recognize and identify vocabulary words. Write vocabulary words on the board. Have students copy these words onto their game boards in random order, one word per box. Use scrap construction paper or buttons for markers. Call out words in random order and instruct students to mark them on their boards until someone gets Bingo.
- Enlarge the cards and have each student draw a picture in each box that represents the definition of a vocabulary word. For example, if students are learning animal words, have them draw one animal in each box. Write the vocabulary words on index cards, show the cards, and have students mark the corresponding boxes.
- Complete the above activity in the opposite manner. Have students copy the vocabulary words onto their Bingo cards, then show a picture of each word. Students should recognize the corresponding word and mark it on their boards.
- Use variations of this game to suit curricular needs. For example, if students are studying opposites, they can draw or write one set of the words on their cards and mark their cards according to the opposites you call. For example, when you say, "small," have students mark boxes containing the word *big*.

Specific Word Instruction: Book Walk

A "book walk" (or "picture walk") happens when students look through pictures in a book before reading it to get ideas about the content. This comprehension strategy can also be used as a vocabulary strategy when implemented in the following manner. First, select critical story vocabulary (words that are essential to the overall theme, unfamiliar words, words that are important for overall comprehension, etc.). Show the cover illustration and title. Explain that a book walk is when students "walk" through the book with their eyes to get an idea of what it will be about. Flip through the book, pause at each page, and discuss what might be happening. As you do this, "implant" the vocabulary words that you have selected. For example, if you want to teach students the animal names in the book *In the Tall, Tall Grass* by Denise Fleming (Henry Holt & Co., 1995), you might say, "What do you see happening on this page? That looks like it might be a type of bird. Maybe it is a hummingbird because I see its wings moving very fast." Then, when students read (or listen to) the story, they will already have been exposed to the vocabulary terms and their meanings.

First-Rate Reading™: Fluency, Vocabulary, Comprehension • CD-104017 • © Carson-Dellosa Basics

Name _____   *Vocabulary*

 Bingo Card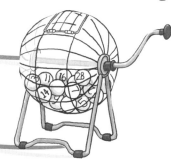

Specific Word Instruction: Vocabulary Charades

Another fun game for vocabulary instruction is Charades, an ideal game for students who learn by moving. Charades can be used with new vocabulary words that can be acted out and to review words learned throughout the year. To play, whisper a vocabulary word in a student's ear and have him act it out for the class to guess. For a more challenging version, let students suggest words to you or each other. To make the game more competitive, form teams and let each student take a turn acting out a vocabulary word as his team guesses. If a team guesses correctly, give them a point. If a team does not guess correctly, allow the other team to guess.

Specific Word Instruction: Teaching Words Prior to Reading

Before reading a story aloud, it is important to teach critical vocabulary words. Write the vocabulary words on the board. Explain that the story contains some new words students should learn before reading. Ask students how they think this might help them understand the story. Discuss each word's meaning. After the discussion, point to each word and read it aloud. Have students repeat it. If possible, ask students if they know what the word means, if they have ever heard of it, if they can use it in a sentence, etc. Then, define the word for students, trying to make it as relevant as possible. For example, if the word is *toppled*, say, "The word *toppled* means *fell*. In the story, the teddy bear *fell*, or *toppled*, off the bed. Have you ever toppled off something?" Let students describe times they toppled.

Specific Word Instruction: Flash Cards

Reinforce new vocabulary words with flash cards. Write words on sets of index cards, then laminate the cards if desired.

- Write each word on one side of an index card and draw a picture definition on the back. Let pairs "play" in a center. Let the first student shuffle the cards and show one to his partner. The partner should read the word and say its meaning, or see the picture and state the word. Then, have students shuffle the cards and switch roles.
- Have students create their own flash cards to use at home. Give each student five index cards on which to copy words and draw pictures. Have students practice reading the cards at home with adults. Consider having students store their cards in resealable, plastic bags to create personal word banks.
- Have students use premade flash cards to play Concentration. Divide the flash cards equally among students and give each student the same number of index cards as he has flash cards. First, have each student copy words from the flash card set onto his index cards. Have pairs of students combine their flash cards and index cards, shuffle them, place them facedown, sort them into rows, then take turns flipping over two cards and reading the vocabulary words. If the words match, the student keeps the pair and goes again. If the words do not match, the student places the cards facedown in their original positions and the second player takes a turn. The student with the most pairs wins. For a more challenging version of this game, have students play using a set of cards containing both the words and their meanings. (Meanings can be depicted with pictures for pre-readers.) Students should then match the words and their meanings.

Specific Word Instruction: Students Predict Possible Vocabulary Words Prior to Reading

This activity requires students to use critical thinking skills as they think about vocabulary and will take some modeling and practice at first. Prior to reading a story or article, give students background information, then ask students to predict words they might find in the text. For example, before reading a book about zoo animals, say, "This book tells about different kinds of animals you might see in a zoo and the noises they make. What are some words that you think we might see in this book?" Guide students toward suggestions, such as *lion, tiger, roar,* etc. As students suggest possible words, write them on the board. Read the book, then revisit the list to see which words were found in the book. The words that were in the story can become the current vocabulary list. The words that were not in the story can spawn a discussion about possible reasons why they were not in the story. For example, you might ask, "Why do you think the predicted word *car* was not in the zoo story?" This discussion helps students think about words and context.

Specific Word Instruction: Guess That Word!

To review vocabulary words and meanings, as well as assess students' understandings of them, play Guess That Word! This game can only be played with words whose meanings can be illustrated. For example, words like *and, the,* and *of* are not good choices, while nouns like *caterpillar, beret,* and *mustache* are easy to draw. Display a list of current, illustratable vocabulary words. Demonstrate how to play the game by being the first player. Select one of the words and draw its meaning on the board. Students must guess the word you are drawing. When a student guesses correctly, let her draw the next word. Students can play as a class if you have them take turns drawing the meanings. The game can also be played in small groups or with partners. To make it more competitive, assign students to teams. Have team members take turns drawing words. If a team guesses a word correctly, they get one point. If they do not guess it correctly, they lose a turn. The game can also be played with a time limit, in which teams must guess as many words as possible within a certain amount of time.

Specific Word Instruction: Student Choice

When students are allowed to make decisions about their learning, they are intrinsically more motivated. Have students choose the vocabulary words they want to learn. First, explain the process and discuss the criteria for word selection. Explain that students can choose words that they would like to learn because they are interesting, new, unfamiliar, confusing, funny, important, etc., as long as they are prepared to discuss why they chose particular words. Read a story aloud and tell students to listen for words they would like to make part of their new vocabulary list. After reading, review each page and have students offer suggestions for the vocabulary list. Write down all choices. When the initial list is complete, guide students toward making final choices to narrow the list. Keep the list short for young students—between five and 10 words, depending on the activities that will be completed with it. Next, initiate discussions about the word choices. For example, if a student suggests the word *grouchy* from the book *The Grouchy Ladybug* by Eric Carle (HarperTrophy, 1996), ask, "Why did you pick *grouchy?*" The student might say, "Because it is in the title," or "Because I don't know what the word means," or even "My mom always says I'm grouchy in the morning!" The next step is to ask probing questions in order to get students to think about the word's meaning and importance to the story. For example, say, "Oh, I see. So, you think that we should use the word *grouchy* because it is in the title. I also noticed that. Do you think the word is important or not-so-important if the author used it in the title? What do you think the word *grouchy* might mean? How do you feel when you are grouchy?"

Specific Word Instruction: Vocabulary Categorization

This critical thinking activity requires students to use words' meanings to categorize them. Students must also think about how words are interrelated. Model higher-level thinking for students until they understand it. Provide a list of words that are obviously related, such as *blue, red, green, black, yellow,* and *orange.* Next to each word, display an object that is traditionally related to that word so that emerging readers can "read" the words. For example, if using color words, color a small area red next to the word *red.* Include one word that is obviously not related, such as *cat.* Read the word list to students and ask, "Which of these words does not belong?" Discuss why the word *cat* does not belong. Extend the activity by asking students to suggest other words that would belong in the group (more color words). Continue with other groups, such as animal names, sounds, school things, names, words related to a current theme or story, etc. For a challenging extension to this activity, have students create lists of related vocabulary words in pairs and challenge the class to discover which word on each list does not belong. Use the Categorization reproducible (page 45) for additional practice. For even more practice, create several lists of obviously related words, such as *dog, cat, bird, tiger, hamster,* and *snake;* and *pencil, desk, eraser, chalkboard, paper,* and *students.* Then, present students with a new word, such as *fish.* Ask, "Where does this word belong?" Have students identify the relationship between the new word and the word groups and determine where the new word belongs (in the animal list). Challenge students to think of another new word that would "fit" in one of the word lists. Use the Vocabulary Set reproducible (page 46) for more practice. Answer Key for page 45: Students should cross out the tennis racket, fish, crayon, and tree. Answer Key for page 46: Students should paste the frog in the first row, blocks in the second row, and the pear in the third row.

44

Categorization

Listen as your teacher reads the word
lists below. Put an X on each word that does not belong.

| 1. basketball | tennis racket | football | baseball |

| 2. lion | dog | fox | fish |

| 3. shirt | shoe | crayon | hat |

| 4. soup | tree | cake | apple |

Vocabulary Set

Listen as your teacher reads the words below. Then, listen as your teacher says the picture names. Color and cut out the pictures. Paste each picture next to the row of words that matches the picture.

cow	bear	snake	
ball	top	doll	
hamburger	spaghetti	cookie	

Specific Word Instruction: Word of the Day

An excellent way to systematically teach new words is with Word of the Day activities. Each day, select one new word to teach students by incorporating it into the existing classroom morning routine. It is important to teach the word in the morning so that students can use and identify it as often as possible during the day. Consider students' levels and vocabulary needs, as well as curricular objectives when choosing the words. Below are suggestions for Word of the Day words and activities:

- For beginning readers, use a simple sight word as the word of the day. (See list on page 28.)
- Expose more advanced readers to more challenging words (*joyful, pleasant, frightened,* etc.).
- Select words that correlate to the current season. For example, during October use words such as *pumpkin, candy, autumn,* etc. During winter, use words like *cold, snow, Christmas, Hanukkah, Kwanzaa, mittens,* etc.
- Use words that correlate to current thematic study. For example, during a thematic unit on dinosaurs, use words such as *extinct, fossil, tyrannosaur,* etc.
- Select words based on a current book or story. For example, while reading *The Very Hungry Caterpillar* by Eric Carle (Philomel, 1983), use words like *cocoon, caterpillar, butterfly, metamorphosis, hungry,* etc.
- Choose words based on lessons for subjects other than language arts. When teaching addition, for example, use words like *add, digit, number, sum,* and *plus*. When teaching about families in social studies, use words like *relatives, parent, brother, sister, grandmother,* etc.
- Even everyday activities and real-life words can be vocabulary choices for Words of the Day. Think about words that students are exposed to on a regular basis, like *restaurant, park, bath, morning, school, television, computer, play,* etc. Although students may hear and say these words often, they may need additional exposure to recognize their written forms.

After selecting vocabulary for a Word of the Day activity, decide how to present the word and engage students. Presentation can be as simple as writing the word and its meaning or a picture definition on the board. Point to the word as you read it aloud and ask students to repeat it. Read and discuss its meaning and ask students to use it in a sentence. Or, instead of using the board, use the Word of the Day reproducible (page 48) to present the word.

The last step is to motivate students to learn, interact with, and use the Word of the Day. Below are some suggestions:

- Tell students to listen for the Word of the Day. When they hear it, they must raise their hands/shout/stomp their feet, etc. Encourage students to use the word during the day as much as possible. Reward students who use the word correctly with stickers or similar treats.
- Ask students to draw simple pictures depicting the word in some way. For example, if the Word of the Day is *joy*, have students draw themselves feeling joyful. Allow students to share their drawings with the class. Consider displaying a different drawing each day alongside the Word of the Day.
- Display the Word of the Day on a bulletin board or word wall. Students can refer to the accumulating words when writing, reading, speaking, etc. When a week has passed, ask volunteers to read and define 10 words. Reward each volunteer for each word he identifies correctly. To make the activity competitive, assign students to teams. Award a point for each word a team identifies correctly.

Name _____   *Vocabulary*

Word of the Day

26, March

THE WORD OF THE DAY IS . . .

Word of the Day: _____

Meaning: _____

_____

Illustration

Word of the Day: _____

Meaning: _____

_____

Illustration

Word Learning Strategies: Using Dictionaries

Even very young students benefit from learning to use reference aids, such as dictionaries. Below are suggestions for introducing kindergartners to using references as a word-learning strategy:

- When reading a story, pause at a new word and tell students that you are not sure what it means. Explain that one way to find out is to look it up in a dictionary. Show students an early reader dictionary or picture dictionary. Explain that this book is called a *dictionary* and that it contains words and their meanings. Have students repeat the word. Tell students that good readers use dictionaries to look up new words. Demonstrate looking up the word by saying, "The word I'm looking for starts with the letter *a*, so I will go to the *a* section of the dictionary." (Look for the word.)

  "Here it is. Let me read what the dictionary says." At this point, read the meaning or show them the picture if using a picture dictionary. Then, say, "Now I can go back to the story and reread the sentence. Now I understand what that word means."

- Explain that a picture dictionary is a book with words in print and their meanings in pictures. Show students the dictionary and let them "look up" words with you. Tell them that they will make a class picture dictionary. Assign each student a letter or letters from the alphabet. For example, if you have 22 students, assign each student one letter and then divide the additional four letters between four students, giving those four students two letters each. Have each student copy his letter in uppercase and lowercase at the top of his paper. Brainstorm words that begin with each letter of the alphabet and list them on the board for students to refer to later. If students suggest words that will be difficult to illustrate, such as *and* for the letter *a*, remind them that the words used must be words they can draw. Then, have each student choose a word from the list that begins with his letter and create a page for that letter for the class dictionary. Tell each student to copy his word and illustrate its meaning. Bind the pages together and add a cover with the title *Our Class Picture Dictionary*.

- Have students create their own mini-dictionaries based on a current theme of study. For example, when studying the seasons, have students create personal dictionaries with seasonal vocabulary words, such as *spring, summer, fall, winter*, etc. For each page, have each student write a word and its definition, draw a picture of it, and use it in a sentence. (Pre-readers can copy the definitions and dictate sentences.) Give each student two additional pieces of paper to create a cover with a title, such as *My Seasons Dictionary*. Bind the books with staples or yarn. Encourage students to practice reading their words, definitions, and sentences. Send books home for students to share.

Word Learning Strategies—Word Parts: Suffixes

Students need to learn how to use word parts to figure out the meanings of words. Help students begin to practice a simple form of structural analysis by explaining that whenever a good reader comes to a word she cannot identify, she can sometimes "break" the word into recognizable pieces. For example, if a student comes to the word *runner* and is unable to read the word, you can guide the student to "break" the word and find *run*. Write the following sentences on the board: *Ben likes to play. He plays outside. Ben is a good player. He played all day. Ben is playing now.* Read the sentences a few times. Ask students what Ben likes to do (play). Ask a student volunteer to come to the board and underline the word *play* in the first sentence. Then, have another student underline the word *plays* in the second sentence. Repeat until all versions of the word are underlined. Ask students what they notice about all of these words. They should notice that they all start with the word *play* but end differently. Rewrite the underlined words on the board (*play, plays, player, played, playing*). Give each student four index cards. Have each student write one letter in the word *play* on each card. Tell each student to "build" the word *play* by putting the letter cards in order. Then, give one more card to each student to label with an *s*. Ask what the word *play* becomes when they add this letter to the word (*plays*). Repeat with additional cards for *-er*, *-ed*, and *-ing*. Ask which letters did not change when they added new endings to the word (*play*). Tell students that the word *play* is the base word, and the endings are called suffixes. Let students practice adding these suffixes to other words and point them out when students come across them in reading.

Word Learning Strategies—Word Parts: Prefixes

Two of the most common prefixes in English are *un-* and *re-*. Because their meanings are clear and easy to learn (*un-* means not and *re-* means again), young students will benefit from learning these prefixes. Write the word *happy* in the middle of a web, and ask students to list some things that make them feel happy. Write their answers around the web. Then, form another web with the word *unhappy* in the middle. Ask them what this word means and have them list some things that make them unhappy. Give each student a piece of construction paper. Tell students to fold the papers in half lengthwise to create two columns, and then write the word *happy* at the top of one column and *unhappy* at the top of the other column. Each student may also add a happy face and an unhappy face to the appropriate columns. Direct each student to draw things that make him happy on the happy side and things that make him unhappy on the unhappy side. Afterward, ask students what they notice about the two headings. (They are the same word except one starts with the prefix *un-*.) Explain that the word *happy* is the base word, *un-* is a prefix, and the prefix *un-* means not. Give other examples of the prefix *un-* in other words, such as *tie/untie, fold/unfold, dress/undress, comfortable/uncomfortable, wind/unwind*, etc. Find words while reading that contain the prefix *un-*. To teach the prefix *re-*, read a passage, story, or sentence. Then, tell students that you will *reread* it, and ask them what that means. If students are not clear, demonstrate by actually rereading it and ask again. Tell students that the word *reread* also contains a base word and a prefix. Ask them to guess which is the base and which is the prefix. (Remind them of the previous lesson with the prefix *un-*.) Tell them that the prefix *re-* means again. Give other examples while reading, such as *rewrite, redo, retie, refold*, etc. Encourage students to find words that contain the prefix *re-*.

World Learning Strategies: Finding Little Words Inside Big Words

Teach young readers to find "little" words inside "big" words to help them figure out new words in text. On index cards, write the letters and words *run, n, i, n, g, play, g, r, o, u, n,* and *d*. Call five students to the front of the room and ask each one to hold a letter card to spell *running*. Tell the class that this is a "big" word and that readers

sometimes get stuck on big words. Good readers, however, look for little words inside of big words to figure them out. Ask students if they can find a little word inside this big word. Because the letters *r, u,* and *n* are on one card, even emerging readers should be able to find this little word. When students identify the word *run*, guide them toward reading the whole word by sounding out each letter. Repeat with the cards that spell *playground*. Extend this activity with the Compound Words activity below.

Word Learning Strategies: Compound Words

Write the following words on sentence strips: *upstairs, grandmother, playground, classroom,* and *basketball*. Display the word *upstairs* on a pocket chart. Ask students how many words are in the pocket (one) and how they know it is only one word. (There is no extra space between any letters.) Cut the sentence strip in half and display *up* and *stairs* with a space between. Ask how many words are now in the pocket chart (two) and have them explain how they know there are two words. (There is space between the

words.) Ask students to use the word *up* in a sentence. Repeat with the word *stairs*. Next, ask each student to use the word *upstairs* in a sentence. Tell students that big words made up of two little words are called *compound words*. Repeat with the remaining sentence strips. Then, have two students stand up separately to hold the sentence strips with *grand* and *mother*. Read the two separate words as a class. Have the two students stand together to form the compound word. Ask the class what new word the two words make. Repeat for the rest of the compound words. Use the Compound Words reproducible (page 52) for additional practice finding little words inside big words.

Compound Words

Listen as your teacher reads the "little" words below. Write each new "big" word on a line. Look at the pictures to get clues. Then, practice reading the new compound words.

sea + shell = _____
_____

tool + box = _____
_____

cup + cake = _____
_____

ham + burger = _____
_____

butter + fly = _____
_____

First-Rate Reading™: Fluency, Vocabulary, Comprehension • CD-104017 • © Carson-Dellosa
Basics

Word Learning Strategies: Context Clues

Context clues are hints a reader can find in the text to help him determine an unknown word. Teach students how to use context and picture clues with actual text (or "in context"), and apply this strategy often when reading in class. Use the following example to demonstrate how to use context clues. Write the word *commotion* on the board. Read it aloud and ask if anyone has heard of this word, can guess what it might mean, etc. Tell students that it is difficult to figure out what a word means when it is "all by itself." But, when a good reader comes to an unknown word in a book, she can use clues (like a detective) to figure it out, even if it is a hard word or a long word like this one. Write the following paragraph on the board: *Mary and Joe wanted to give the dog a bath. Spot did not want to take a bath. He jumped out of the tub and started running all over the house. He left water and soap everywhere! Mary and Joe yelled and screamed as they chased Spot down the stairs. Mother was not happy when she heard all of this commotion.* Although the passage is above a typical kindergarten reading level, having the text on the board as you read it aloud and discuss it will help students see the connection between thinking about vocabulary and looking at the actual print. Read the sentences aloud and tell students to imagine this happening in their own houses: chasing, running, yelling, getting soap and water everywhere, etc. Then, say, "I know from the sentences that there is a lot of craziness going on. The dog is running everywhere, all wet and soapy. The children are chasing him and yelling and screaming. I can tell that the word *commotion* might mean a lot of noise and confusion."

Word Learning Strategies: Picture Clues

A picture clue is another type of context clue that gives hints a reader can use to help him determine an unknown word. To teach students to use picture clues, show this simple drawing of a boy on a skateboard. On the board, write *Steven went outside to ride his skateboard.* Read the sentence aloud and pretend to get "stuck" on the word *skateboard*. Tell students that you can use the picture to get a clue about what the word might mean. Think aloud, saying, "I will look at the picture to see if I can get a clue. I see a boy. He is on a skateboard. Let me try reading the sentence again to see if the word might be *skateboard*. Yes, the word starts with the letter *s* and the sentence makes sense. Steven went outside to ride his skateboard."

Vocabulary Assessments

Even though many kindergartners are pre-readers, there are still ways to assess their beginning vocabulary skills. Informal assessment can occur whenever you hear a student use a new word in conversation or see her write it. To set up an informal, conversational assessment, arrange a quiet area in the classroom and have conversations with individual students while their classmates are working independently. Check for specific vocabulary acquisition by planning the conversations beforehand. Include key words students should know. Keep a mental or written running record of which words students understand when you say them or when students use the words themselves. For example, if students are learning about colors, talk with students about their favorite and least favorite colors, have them discuss rainbows, differences in crayon names, and colorful clothing. (Wear colorful clothing that day!) Keep a checklist of the color words that is abbreviated or hidden, so that students will not use the list as a prompt. Mark each word a student uses or understands.

Take more formal vocabulary assessments to help students learn and remember new vocabulary. Formal assessments can start at a level suitable for pre-readers. Use the Vocabulary Assessment #1 reproducible (page 55) throughout the year to encourage pre-readers to learn new words, even if they cannot yet write them. This assessment is also good for classifying pre-writers, since some students will only be able to draw definitions. Before the assessment, choose three words that are easy to illustrate and write them on the reproducible. Then, give each student a copy of the reproducible, call out each word, and have students draw pictures to show what the words mean. Allow students to add written definitions if they are capable. This will show which students can write and which students are still pre-writers.

Vocabulary assessments should become more writing-focused as students' reading and writing skills improve. The Vocabulary Assessment #2 reproducible (page 56) can be used in a variety of ways. You may choose to give students words and have them write definitions, even if students must use invented spelling or dictation to do so. Or, you can write definitions and have them fill in words. Finally, you can choose a compromise between the two, writing some words and some definitions and having students fill in what is needed.

Finally, let students use the Vocabulary Assessment #2 reproducible (page 56) as a fun practice tool. Be sure to add directions if necessary.

- After reading a new book aloud, reread it and ask students to stop you when you come to a word they do not know. Help them define the word using context and picture clues. Put the words on a word wall and write them on the reproducible for students to illustrate.
- Send students on a scavenger hunt for new words. Have students walk around the room and choose objects for which they would like to learn the corresponding word. Write each chosen word on an index card and post the card next to the object. Let each student choose three words to copy and illustrate on the reproducible.
- Play Stump the Teacher. Send a copy of the reproducible home with each student, along with a note to families asking that they help students find three new words. Instruct each student to draw the definitions on the reproducible, write the words on a separate piece of paper, and return the reproducible to you. For "homework" one night, try to guess each new word and write the words on the reproducibles. Return papers for students to check your work, or check them as a class.

Name _____   *Vocabulary*

Date _____

Vocabulary Assessment #1

Listen to your teacher read the words. In
each box, draw a picture of the word or write the definition.

1. _____

2. _____

3. _____

Name _____

Date _____

Vocabulary

Vocabulary Assessment #2

Your teacher will tell you what to
draw and write in the boxes below.

1. _____

2. _____

3. _____

First-Rate Reading™: Fluency, Vocabulary, Comprehension • CD-104017 • © Carson-Dellosa
Basics

Comprehension

Pre-Reading Strategies: Introduction

It is critical to teach students strategies they can implement before reading. Emerging readers need to learn how to use book covers, titles, pictures, etc., to improve their comprehension as well as natural reading behaviors, such as previewing, predicting, etc. These reading strategies are simple yet effective in aiding comprehension.

Pre-Reading Strategies: Preview

Many young readers will simply open a book to the first page and begin reading without the benefits of previewing. Previewing is critical for emerging readers because they need to learn what to look for when choosing books and also because it will help them understand the books they choose. Show a picture book and ask students to describe what they see on the cover. Explain that these pictures will give them clues about the text. Have them guess what the book will be about. Write their guesses on the board, then read the title aloud to students, noting that the title will also give a big clue about the story. Ask students to make new guesses based on the pictures and the title. Write these guesses below the previous ones. Next, tell students that sometimes the back of a book will have a summary or blurb about the book. Read the blurb if there is one, ask students to guess again, and record these guesses. Finally, explain that looking through the pages will also tell about the story. Flip through the book, pausing at any pictures. Ask students to guess again and record these guesses, also. Tell students that this is called *previewing*, and it helps their brains "get ready" to read, understand, and enjoy the text more. After reading the story, revisit the guesses. Discuss the accuracy of the guesses and whether they helped students understand the story and know what to expect. Compare the accuracy of the last set of guesses—which were based on the pictures, title, blurb, and looking through the book—with the first guesses, which were only based on the cover's pictures. Be sure to preview when reading books throughout the year.

Pre-Reading Strategies: Set the Purpose for Reading

Students' comprehension increases when they read with a set purpose. You can set a purpose for students in several ways, depending on the reading material and academic objective. One simple way to set the purpose for reading is through making predictions. The purpose for reading can also be based on the reading material. For example, if students will read a science article about plants, state, "Our purpose for reading this article is to find out how a seed turns into a plant." If students will read a story about a little girl who gets a puppy, the purpose might be, "We will read this story to find out what happens when a little girl gets a puppy." Orally set the purpose as described above or set it during a class discussion by asking why students want to read the story. Always tell students to keep their purposes in mind while reading and revisit their purposes after reading.

Pre-Reading Strategies: Predictions

Predicting is a simple but powerful reading strategy that helps the reader comprehend text by giving him something to look for. A prediction can be as simple as asking students what they think the story will be about. It can also be more complex, requiring them to think about more specific questions. For example, if students listen to a story about a little girl who gets a puppy, guide them to make predictions by asking, "How do you think the little girl feels when she gets the puppy? Do you think the puppy will like the little girl? What do you think will happen after the little girl gets the puppy?" Predicting cannot occur without previewing, and predictions naturally set a purpose for reading because a reader wants to know if his prediction is right or wrong. Students must understand that predictions are about helping them understand the story, not about being right or wrong. Young students may hesitate to guess for fear of being wrong, but they need to be imaginative in making predictions and thinking about the possibilities of a story line.

Additionally, young readers tend to predict very superficially. For example, for the above story, a student might say, "I think the story will be about a dog." Model forming detailed predictions by saying things like, "I also think this story will be about a dog. I predict that the dog will be unhappy in his home and will run away. What do you think the story will say about the dog?" Detailed predictions force students to be more thoughtful and also help them identify details in the text. Predictions can be made orally or in writing, but allow students to revisit their predictions during and after reading to confirm or reject them. Below are more specific suggestions for prediction activities.

- Record students' story predictions and revisit them after reading. First, show the cover and read the title. Briefly state what the story is about. For example, when reading *Green Eggs and Ham* by Dr. Seuss (Random House, 1960), explain that the book's main character does not want to try green eggs and ham because he does not think he will like them. Ask students to predict whether he will try them. Record the total number for each guess on the board. After reading the book, revisit the guesses and discuss how many matched the story. Or, ask students to make more specific predictions about what will happen in the story. Write a few predictions on the board with the names of students who made the predictions. After reading, revisit and discuss the predictions.
- Direct each student to illustrate his prediction about what will happen in the book. Tell students to save these for later. After reading the book, have students share what they predicted in their illustrations. For example, when reading *If You Give a Moose a Muffin* by Laura Joffe Numeroff (Scott Foresman, 1991), instruct students to draw pictures of what they think will happen if and when the moose gets the muffin. Compare predictions to what actually happens.
- Help students make personal connections when predicting by asking them to use prior knowledge. For example, when reading *In the Tall, Tall Grass* by Denise Fleming (Henry Holt & Company, 1995), have students think of things they have seen in grass and predict what is in the book based on these experiences.
- Use the Predictions reproducible (page 59) to record students' predictions and review a story's actual content. After previewing, have students write or dictate what they think the story will be about and draw pictures of it. After reading, have students circle whether their predictions were right, kind of right, or wrong, and draw pictures of what the story was really about. Remind students that being right is not important and discuss how predictions helped individual students understand what they are reading.

First-Rate Reading™: Fluency, Vocabulary, Comprehension • CD-104017 • © Carson-Dellosa
Basics

Name _____ *Comprehension*

Predictions

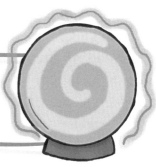

Book Title: _____

I predict that the book will be about _____

_____

_____

Draw what you think will happen in the box below.

[ ]

My prediction was: right.   kind of right.   wrong.

Draw what really happened in the story in the box below.

[ ]

Pre-Reading Strategies: Take a Picture Walk

This strategy requires students to look through a book before reading it to get clues about the story from the pictures. Before reading, tell students that good readers sometimes look through a book's pages to get an idea of what will happen in the story. For example, when reading *The Very Hungry Caterpillar* by Eric Carle (Putnam, 1983), as you turn the pages, pause and say, "I see that on this page there is a caterpillar. He looks like he is waking up." Ask different students to narrate what they think is happening on each page as they look at the pictures. Point out details to help them. For example, say, "The caterpillar doesn't look like he feels very well on this page. Look at his face. Do you think he ate too much and has a stomachache?" Encourage students to do this independently when they read new books.

Pre-Reading Strategies: Journaling

Have students complete journal entries on a topic related to the reading material in order to have them set a purpose for reading, think about the topic, access prior knowledge, and make personal connections with the story. Adding a writing element will help students make personal connections prior to reading, which will increase their comprehension. Journaling can be done in an actual notebook or on loose-leaf paper bound between construction paper covers. The journal topic can be very open-ended, such as, "This story is about a girl who gets a special birthday present. Write about a time you received a special present." When the journal entries are complete, have students share with each other or the class. Consider having students write new journal entries after completing the reading. Students may use invented spelling or dictation to complete their journal entries. If students are not yet ready to use invented spelling and dictation is not feasible, students may illustrate their journal entries.

Pre-Reading Strategies: Webbing

A web is an excellent graphic organizer that helps students access and assess prior knowledge about a text's topic. For example, when reading a book about plant growth, activate students' prior knowledge about the topic by brainstorming web-style prior to reading. Make a transparency of the Webbing reproducible (page 61) or copy it on the board. Ask, "What do you know about how plants grow?" Then, web their responses. Have students select some ideas from the web and copy them onto blank pieces of paper in a web format to get a feel for the exercise. After modeling this for students, give them a chance to complete webs about their own topics using copies of the reproducible. You may wish to review the webs in order to assess students' existing knowledge about the topic and adjust further instruction accordingly. Webs can be revisited during and after reading in order to add newly acquired information.

Webbing

Write or draw your topic in the middle oval. Write or draw related ideas in the other ovals.

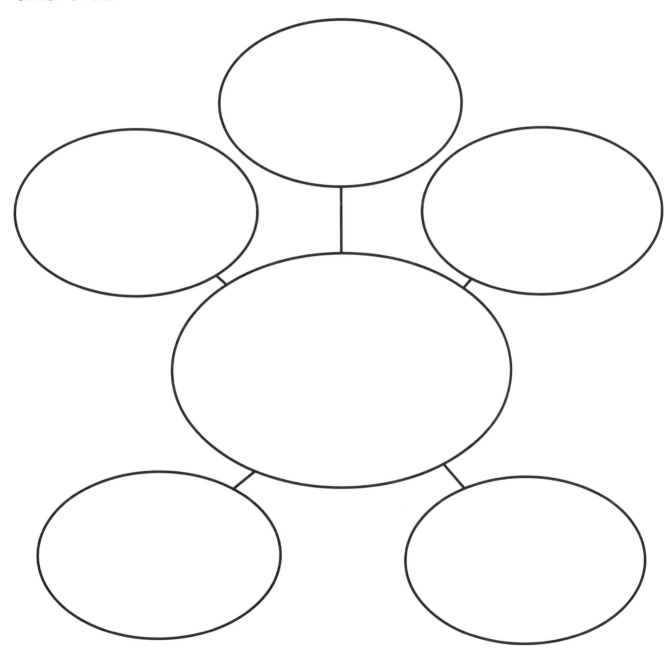

Monitoring Comprehension: Buddy Brains

This simple sharing strategy helps students read actively and monitor their comprehension. Tell students that because two brains are better than one, they will be using their buddies' brains while reading. Assign partners. To model sharing, say, "Turn to your buddy and tell him your favorite color." Have young students practice listening. During pre-reading activities, ask students to silently make predictions about the reading, then have them share predictions with their buddies. As you read, pause occasionally and have students turn to their buddies to discuss their thoughts. For example, while reading *Where the Wild Things Are* by Maurice Sendak (HarperCollins, 1988), pause after Max gets sent to bed without supper and ask students to think of times when they were punished. Then, have students turn to their buddies and share memories. As students turn to their buddies repeatedly to quickly respond to, interact with, or answer questions about the reading, they will actively listen throughout the reading.

Monitoring Comprehension: What Do I Know So Far?

Help students monitor their comprehension in small, manageable steps. Explain that good readers make sure they understand what they are reading as they read. While reading, students should ask themselves, "What do I know so far?" every few pages. After reading the first couple of pages of *Where the Wild Things Are* by Maurice Sendak (HarperCollins, 1988), pause and say, "What do I know so far?" Answer aloud, "The story is about a boy named Max who got in trouble for being wild. He was sent to his room without supper." Pause after a few more pages and ask, "What do you know so far?" Help students summarize the events. Repeat for every few pages. At the end, ask students to retell the story. Ask if pausing to answer this question helped them understand. Explain that if students cannot answer this question at any point, they should reread parts of the book. For practice, have students independently monitor their comprehension as you read. Give each student a piece of paper. Determine how often and when you will pause while reading, then have students fold their papers to create that many sections. For example, if you will pause to ask, "What do you know so far?" four times, help students fold and unfold their papers into four sections. Then, have them illustrate their answers to the question each time you stop during the reading.

Monitoring Comprehension: "Brain TV" and Visualization

Teach young readers how to visualize what they are reading in order to monitor their own comprehension. To help each student learn this strategy, tell her that she should see the action happening in her mind, like on a television screen. Compare a "Brain TV" to a television screen. Have students close their eyes and "see" or visualize what you describe. Then, describe a simple, detailed scene, such as, "You are in the park. The sky is bright blue. The sun is hot and bright. There are children all around you, playing and laughing and running and sliding down the slide." Next, have students open their eyes and share what they "saw" on their Brain TVs. After students understand this, select a story scene with action and detail. Read it several times. Encourage students to close their eyes again if they prefer. Then, give students paper and tell them to draw what they visualized, including as many details as possible in their illustrations. Let students share their work, and discuss the differences and similarities in the illustrations. Display the scenes on a bulletin board titled "We Use Our Brain TVs When We Read!" Remind students to "turn on" their Brain TVs when you begin a new story.

Using Graphic and Semantic Organizers: Beginning, Middle, End

Help students differentiate parts of a story. Model the strategy with a familiar book that has distinct parts. Write the column headings *Beginning, Middle,* and *End* on the board. Read the book aloud and ask, "What happened at the beginning?" Record responses and repeat for the other two sections. Next, give students copies of the Beginning, Middle, End reproducible (page 64). Read a new story aloud, then reread the beginning and ask students to draw or write about what happened at the beginning. Repeat for the middle and end. Collect students' papers and cut them into three sections. Divide a bulletin board into three sections, label them to match the reproducible sections, and post student work in the appropriate sections. Repeat with other new books for practice.

Using Graphic and Semantic Organizers: Story Map

Get students moving as you teach them to recognize simple story elements, such as characters, setting, and plot. Copy a large version of the Story Map reproducible (page 65) on the board. Read a story aloud. After reading, ask a volunteer to name one character. Write the character on the board and have that student stand at the front of the classroom. (Students will see this as a reward and will want to participate.) Ask another volunteer to name another character, then allow that volunteer to stand with the other student. Continue until all characters are listed. Then, ask additional volunteers to name details about the setting and join their classmates at the front of the classroom. Repeat with details about the plot. Continue to let students add details until all are standing. The next time you share a story, let students draw or write details on their own copies of the reproducible.

Using Graphic and Semantic Organizers: Main Idea and Summary

Teaching students to recognize the main idea in a piece of writing at an early age helps them fine-tune this skill later with more complex pieces of writing. Preview a story, then read it aloud. Write the title on the Main Idea and Summary reproducible (page 66), then give a copy to each student. Ask students to illustrate the "biggest" thing that happened in the story. Then, if students can write, ask them to list a few words to go with their pictures. Collect the reproducibles and use them to assess students' grasp of the concept of main idea.

Using Graphic and Semantic Organizers: Book Review

The purpose of analyzing a text is to use that knowledge to form an opinion. On a Web site that sells children's books, look up a few you have recently read to students. Print out several book reviews. Reread one book aloud, then read the reviews. Ask students if they agree or disagree with the reviews. Then, distribute copies of the Book Review reproducible (page 67). Help them fill out responses. Explain that they are learning how to choose books they like. To extend the activity, send home copies of the reproducible with a note to families asking them to let their children dictate reviews about favorite (or least favorite) books. Have students bring the books to class and share the reviews. Label the books with students' names and place them in a temporary library. Post reviews for students to read in order to decide which books to read.

Beginning, Middle, End

Draw each part of the story. Then,
write a sentence or a few words to explain
each drawing.

Beginning

Middle

End

First-Rate Reading™: Fluency, Vocabulary, Comprehension • CD-104017 • © Carson-Dellosa
Basics

Story Map

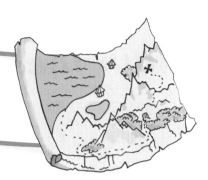

Fill in the boxes below using words
and pictures.

Who was in the story?

Where did the story happen?

What was the story about?

Main Idea and Summary

Write the story title, then follow the
directions below.

Story Title: _____

Draw the "biggest" thing that happened in the story.

Write a few words to go with your picture. _____

_____

_____

_____

First-Rate Reading™: Fluency, Vocabulary, Comprehension • CD-104017 • © Carson-Dellosa
Basics

Book Review

Circle a face below to tell how much
you liked or disliked the book.

Use the lines below to write why you felt that way.

_____

_____

_____

_____

Draw a picture in the box to show why you felt that way.

Answering and Generating Comprehension Questions: Teaching the Difference Between Lower- and Higher-Order Questions

Defining higher- and lower-order questions for students is a simplified way of explaining the different types of questions used in QAR, which stands for Question-Answer Relationships, an idea developed by Taffy Raphael [Raphael, Taffy. "Teaching Question-and-Answer Relationships, Revisited." *Reading Teacher* 39(6): 516-522 (1986)]. Lower-order questions have answers that can be found explicitly in the text, while higher-order questions require students to think critically in order to supply answers. Although the concept is abstract, emerging readers can begin to understand the difference and benefit from exposure to higher-order questions, which make the reader interact with text, infer, and think critically. Many young readers have only been exposed to lower-order questions, which require little thinking and much searching through text.

To teach students the difference between these types of questions, begin with examples of the terms *higher* and *lower*. For example, ask, "Which is harder—the higher level of a video game or the lower level? Which is harder—being in a higher grade, like fifth, or being in a lower grade, like kindergarten?" Tell students that some reading questions are like that, too. Some are higher because they need to have their brains on "high power," while some are lower because they can have their brains on "low power." Demonstrate this with a familiar book. For example, if students are reading *The Napping House* by Audrey Wood (Red Wagon Books, 2000), first tell them to turn their brains on low power because they will be answering some lower-order questions about the story. Ask,

"Who is napping in the napping house? What time of day is it? Who fell asleep last?" Guide students to answer each question and point out how the answers are right in the story. Ask students to comment on whether the questions were hard to answer. Then, tell students to turn their brains to high power in order to answer higher-order questions that will make them think harder. Explain that the answers will not be word-for-word in the text of the story. Ask, "What do you think the grandma was dreaming about? What would you do if you were woken suddenly in the middle of a nap? What do you think the characters did after they all woke up? Why do you think everyone got in the same bed?" As students answer these questions, point out how their answers might vary because the answers to these questions are not in the book. Even though they refer to the book, students have to think about their answers. Repeat these discussions when you answer questions about other reading material. Use the terms higher and lower often so that students get used to them and become more familiar with them for future grade levels.

Generating and Answering Comprehension Questions

Students benefit from learning how to create their own questions. First, if they understand the thinking process required to create a question, they can go through the thinking process required to answer a question. Second, generating questions requires critical and higher-order thinking. Finally, generating questions requires students to reconsider the text. After students have demonstrated an adequate understanding of the difference between lower- and higher-order questions (see page 68), challenge them to create their own questions, either as a whole group or in small groups. (Kindergartners should not be expected to generate questions independently; rather, they should simply be exposed to the thinking process.) Review higher- and lower-order questions, then help students create questions about a familiar text, such as, *The Napping House* by Audrey Wood (Red Wagon Books, 2000). First, ask, "What lower-order question can I ask a reader about the story?" Then, think aloud as you create a simple question based on the text: "I know that the answer to a lower-order question can be found right in the story. It says on this page that there is a grandma in a napping house. I can make up a question that asks, 'Who is the first character sleeping in the napping house?' What is the answer to that question?" After students answer, repeat the process, soliciting help and suggestions from students. When students understand how to create lower-order questions, move to higher-order questions. (Remind students that they may use their own unanswered questions about the text for this exercise.) Initiate these discussions many times, then challenge groups to create questions about the text for classmates to answer. Model the Question Generating reproducible (page 70) prior to having students complete it. If students have difficulty writing, work in small groups or have students dictate their questions to you.

Answering and Generating Questions: Comprehension Games

Use these games to encourage young students to practice answering comprehension questions about current texts.
* Stand in a circle with students. Toss a ball of yarn to a student. When he catches it, ask a comprehension question about the text. If he answers correctly, have him toss the ball to someone else in the circle as he holds on to the end of the yarn. If he answers incorrectly, he should throw the ball back to you and release the end of the yarn. As you ask more questions, have other students toss the ball and hold on to the yarn to create a spiderweb.
* Have students stand up by their desks. Go around the room and ask each child a question about the text. If the student answers correctly, she should remain standing. If she answers incorrectly, she is "out" and should sit. Continue until one student is standing and is the winner. Questions can progress in difficulty as you go around the room a second time.
* Assign students to teams of five. Ask each team a different comprehension question. The team members should confer about their answers. If they answer correctly, they get a point. If they do not, let the next team try to answer for a point. The team with the most points wins.
* Play Comprehension Bingo. Create 12 text-based questions that require one-word or one-phrase answers. Write the answers only on the board. If necessary, add a simple picture to each answer to help students read them. Give each student a copy of the Bingo Card reproducible (page 41). Have students copy the answers on their cards in random order. Then, ask the corresponding questions. Students should mark the answers on their cards with paper scraps or buttons. The first student to get five squares in a row should call out, "Bingo!" Check answers to make sure the student is correct.

Question Generating ?

Book Title: _____

Write a question about the characters in the story. _____

_____

_____ ?

Answer: _____

_____

_____

Write a question about what happened in the story. _____

_____

_____ ?

Answer: _____

_____

_____

First-Rate Reading™: Fluency, Vocabulary, Comprehension • CD-104017 • © Carson-Dellosa

Basics

Recognizing Story Structure: Sequencing

Give emerging readers a concrete way to practice recognizing the sequence of story structure by using actual objects. Prepare the following items: a cookie, a cookie with a bite taken out of it, a half-eaten cookie, and cookie crumbs. (Or, enlarge the drawing at right and cut apart the objects.) Place the items on paper plates in the order listed. Ask students to describe why these things are "in order." Then, ask students to put the following items in order: an unsharpened pencil, a sharpened pencil, a half-used pencil with a partially used eraser, and a pencil nub. Discuss sequencing and how they knew in what order to place the items. Tell students that stories have order, or sequence, too. Things that happen in a story occur in a logical order that makes sense. Explain that good readers look for sequence when reading. Use the Sequencing reproducible (page 72) to help students become more familiar with sequencing, then have them apply the skill with several familiar stories. Students can identify sequence through discussion, by completing the Beginning, Middle, End reproducible (page 64), or by drawing the events in order.

Recognizing Story Structure: Is It Real or Fantasy?

The word *genre* means the category of text (fiction, nonfiction, fantasy, poetry, etc.). To introduce the concept of genres to young students, initiate a lesson comparing real and make-believe (or fantasy) elements in a story. Use a text that has both fantastic and realistic elements, such as *Where the Wild Things Are* by Maurice Sendak (HarperCollins, 1988). Explain that the words *realistic* and *real* mean that an event could really happen while the word *fantasy* means that an event could never happen—it is make-believe. Flip through the book, review the main events, and ask students to name things that could be real or are realistic. (Focus on one element at a time to avoid confusing students.) For example, say, "What about Max wearing a wolf suit? Is that something that could happen in real life? Could a child in a costume be real?" List the responses on the board under the column heading *Real*. Then, read the book, this time looking for fantasy elements and writing them under the heading *Fantasy*. Repeat the activity with other books. After finishing the chart, have students complete copies of the Real or Fantasy? reproducible (page 73).

Name _____

Sequencing

Cut out the picture cards. Paste
each set in the correct order on a sheet of paper.

First-Rate Reading™: Fluency, Vocabulary, Comprehension • CD-104017 • © Carson-Dellosa
Basics

Name _____   *Comprehension*

Real or Fantasy?

Book Title: _____

Find something in the book that could be real. Find something that is fantasy. Draw pictures of your two ideas.

Real

Fantasy

Recognizing Story Structure: Genre Study

When students have mastered the difference between real and fantasy (page 71), teach them about genres. Remind students that *genres* are the categories of literature and reading material. It is important for students to learn how to distinguish between genres because they can then recognize literary patterns. Although literature can be divided into more complex genres than those included here, these categories are appropriate for kindergarten students. Display an enlarged copy of the Genre Chart reproducible (page 75) when teaching genres. First, make the idea of categorization concrete for students by asking the boys to stand on one side of the room and the girls to stand on the other. Ask, "How have I divided the class into groups?" Repeat with other categories, such as hair color, clothing color,

height, table numbers, etc. Tell students that books can be divided into groups too, called *genres*. Review fantasy and real elements to help with the explanation of the reproducible, then read each genre's name and description. Show familiar stories and books as examples of each genre. Assign students to small groups and give each group a familiar book from a different genre. Let each group search their book for proof of the type of genre it is. Instruct group members to agree on the book's genre and be prepared to support their choice with an explanation. Model by showing a book, such as *The Cat in the Hat* by Dr. Seuss (Random House, 1957), and say, "I think this book is fantasy because it has a talking cat and a talking fish. I know these things could never really happen!"

Summarizing: Chain of Events

An excellent way to summarize story events in order is to actually create a chain with paper links so that students see the connection and order of this reading skill. Give each student several strips of construction paper. (The exact number will depend on how many main events occur in the particular book you are using, so decide beforehand how many times you will pause during the reading so that students can identify an event.) Help students work to identify the chain of events in a story. Explain that *events* are the important things that happen in a story. The events of a story are all connected because one makes another one happen, which is why they are called a *chain*. To demonstrate this, display a row of standing dominoes and ask students to predict what will happen when you tip one over. Select a fiction book that has a clear chain of events or choose a nonfiction text that describes a process, such as the life cycle of a butterfly. As you read the book aloud, pause after each main event and allow a few minutes for each student to draw what happened on a paper strip. Be sure students keep their strips in order until you finish reading and they finish drawing all of the main events. Then, have each student glue the strips together to form a paper "chain of events." Hang the chains around the room.

Name _____

Comprehension

Genre Chart

Refer to this chart to help you
remember the differences between the three genres.

Fantasy	Make-believe, could never really happen	 ANIMAL PARTY
Real	Real things that could really happen	 Birthday with Bugsy!
Informational	Teaches facts	 How Flowers Grow

First-Rate Reading™: Fluency, Vocabulary, and Comprehension • CD-104017 • © Carson-Dellosa
Basics

Summarizing: Inferring

Teach this critical thinking skill using concrete examples. Tell students that sometimes readers need to be detectives by using clues to figure things out for themselves. (Students will enjoy learning that the "fancy, teacher word" for this is *inferring*!) Read the following sentence aloud and tell students to use the clues to figure something out, or infer: *Ali's teeth were chattering. Ali was shivering. He put on his coat. Ali was _____ .* Discuss how students were able to infer, or figure out, that Ali was cold. Ask what clues they used. Repeat with the following sentence: *The neighbor's dog always growls at people. He steals my puppy's toys. He even chases the mail carrier! The neighbor's dog is _____* (mean, not friendly). Give students additional practice with inferring using text in class.

Summarizing: Readers' Theater/Dramatization

An excellent and fun way to practice summarizing is through readers' theater and other types of dramatization. Explain that each of these methods is simply a way of retelling main events in a story.

- Use a flannel board with patterns to retell the story.
- Make puppets or masks and retell the story in a play format.
- Have students act out the story without speaking (pantomime). Challenge them to be descriptive enough for the class to be able to "follow along."
- Assign students to read different characters, or parts. Act as the narrator or let a very proficient reader be the narrator. Let the "actors" speak for the characters.
- Have students work in small groups to create simple puppets and retell the story as a puppet show.

Summarizing: Flap Books

Flap books are good, concrete tools to summarize key story elements in fiction. Use the Flap Book reproducible (page 77) to summarize characters, setting, problem, and solution. Have each student cut out the pattern, fold the pattern in half on the gray line, and cut on the dotted lines. Instruct her to summarize the story elements by drawing each element under the flap. Model the completion of each section when first using this activity. Explain each element as follows:

Characters: WHO is in the story?

Setting: WHERE does the story happen?

Problem: WHAT is happening in the story? WHAT is the problem?

Solution: HOW is the problem solved? HOW does the story end?

Post the completed flap books on a bulletin board. Consider creating new flap books each time you begin a new book with students.

Flap Book

Cut out the pattern. Fold on the gray line
so that the words are outside. Then, cut the dashed lines inside the
pattern. Your teacher will tell you what to draw under the flaps.

Characters

Setting

Problem

Solution

Comprehension Assessments

Any comprehension activity a student completes is a form of assessment because it measures whether he understands an individual text. However, it is useful to complete more formal assessments in order to see whether students recognize and can use different strategies. Use these activities and the Comprehension Assessments #1 and #2 (pages 79 and 80) to ensure students are learning how to understand what they read. Be sure to review the instructions on each reproducible as a class.

- After reviewing all pre-reading strategies with students, assign them to small groups. Give each group a book that is not familiar to them, crayons, and a large piece of paper. Ask each group to work together to choose one pre-reading strategy (previewing, setting a purpose, predicting, taking a picture walk, journaling, or webbing), and write or draw steps for using that strategy with the book. When students have chosen their strategies and drawn the steps, spend a few minutes with each group and have them demonstrate the strategy. To make the activity more focused, assign different strategies to different groups or give all groups the same strategy as you teach each one.

- To assess how well students are monitoring their comprehension, plan to read aloud a new book. Give each student a piece of paper and have her divide it into three sections. Read the first part of the book. Then, stop and ask students to write or draw the main events that have happened in the first section. Repeat for the middle and last sections, have students write their names on their papers, then collect and evaluate the papers for comprehension.

- Even very young students can usually learn to complete the most simple graphic organizers. On the lines on the Comprehension Assessment #1 reproducible (page 79), write two subjects with some overlapping information, such as cats and dogs, breakfast and lunch, baseball and soccer, etc. Give each student or small group a copy of the reproducible. Have students fill in the Venn diagrams by writing or drawing things that the subjects have in common in the overlapping section, and writing or drawing things that are different about each subject in the outer portion of the diagram. Evaluate how many characteristics are listed and whether they are in the right places on the diagrams.

- For a simple assessment of question generating, read a big book to students. Ask several lower-order questions and let students take turns coming to the front of the classroom and pointing to the answers in the book. Then, ask several higher-order questions. Let the whole class work together to decide what parts of the text could help them answer it.

- Assess students' awareness of real versus fantasy. Give each student a copy of the Comprehension Assessment #2 reproducible (page 80). If a picture could be real, have the student circle *real* below the box. If it is make-believe, have him circle *fantasy* below the box.

- Read or have students read a short story. On the board, write the question words *who, what, where, when, why,* and *how* (or as many as apply to the story). Have them copy these words onto separate pieces of paper. As a class, brainstorm a question for each question word. Then, have each student write or draw the answer to each question as it applies to the story. Collect the papers. If a student cannot answer any of the questions about the story, have him reread it and try again.

First-Rate Reading™: Fluency, Vocabulary, Comprehension • CD-104017 • © Carson-Dellosa
Basics

Name _____   *Comprehension*

Date _____

Comprehension Assessment #1

Write or draw things that are different
about the subjects in the outside parts of the circles. Write things that
are the same in the part that overlaps.

1. _____

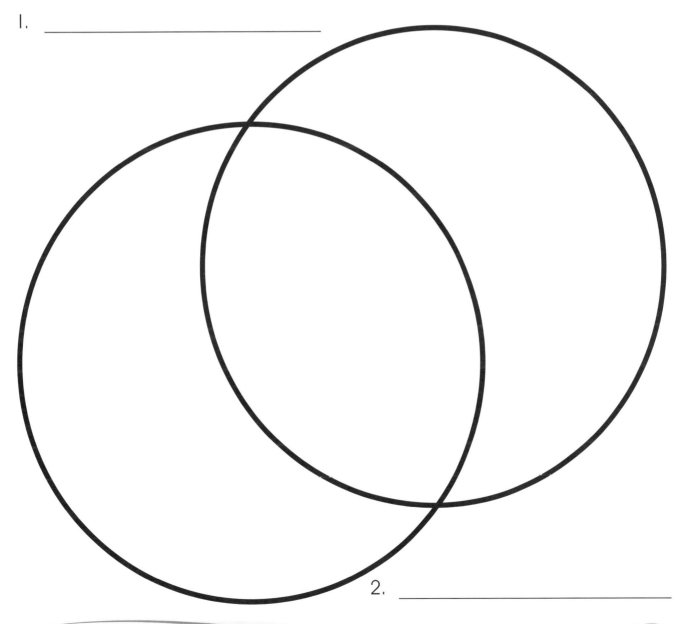

2. _____

Comprehension Assessment #2

Circle the word *real* below the pictures
that could be real. Circle the word *fantasy* below the pictures that could
not be real.

real   fantasy

real   fantasy

real   fantasy

real   fantasy

real   fantasy

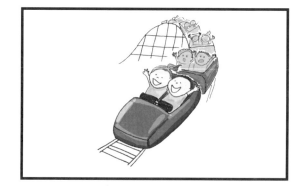

real   fantasy

First-Rate Reading™: Fluency, Vocabulary, Comprehension • CD-104017 • © Carson-Dellosa
Basics